Serenity

RABBI ZELIG PLISKIN

Formulas, stories and insights

Table of Contents

Introduction

*I*magine how wonderful it would be if you could learn to be consistently serene. Serenity is emotional freedom and a general sense of well-being. It is a calm state of mind and body. When you are serene, your brain functions at its optimal level and you think at your best. Serenity is conducive for health and for recovery. Even a tiny bit of serenity is precious.

As you will read in this book, serenity is a learnable skill. What does it take? Knowledge of thought patterns and techniques that create serenity. And then a resolution to serenely review them and put them into practice. Since serenity is a state you create in your mind, only you can create your own serenity. This book, however, can supply you with ideas to integrate and tools to apply.

The Hebrew word for serenity is *menuchas hanefesh*. From a Torah perspective, peace of mind and serenity are essential. We need serenity to concentrate when we pray, to concentrate when we study, to perform good deeds with joy, and to interact harmoniously with others. The only way we can experience unconditional love for other people is by having inner peace ourselves (see Rabbi Yeruchem Levovitz; *Daas Chochmah Umussar*, vol. 2, p. 203). The essence of Shabbos is a day of inner peace and serenity. This adds a positive dimension throughout the entire week. With serenity you will be able to elevate yourself spiritually. Connecting with the Creator is a serene experience.

Everyone alive has challenges that easily create states of stress and anxiety: worries, fears, disappointments, frustration, self-consciousness, feelings of inferiority, nervousness, a lack of confidence, self-pity, blaming and complaining, a feeling of not accomplishing enough, comparing oneself unfavorably with others, health issues, obsessions, a concern with disapproval, a feeling that time is running out, a lack of organization, failures, discouragement, regrets, ideals not lived up to, obstacles to achieving our goals, financial pressures, the problems or suffering of those one cares about, those one finds difficult to get along with, disagreements and quarrels, and the list goes on. Anyone experiencing any of these on a regular basis, and most people do in some fashion, would benefit from an increased level of serenity.

A person who only recently had begun to experience serenity told me, "I had always considered myself to be someone who is naturally anxious and stressed out. I used to think it would be impossible for me to become serene. Fortunately I was mistaken. It's amazing how serenity has made such a major impact on my life. I feel better than I've ever felt before. My mind is clear. I concentrate better and remember more. Not that much has changed in my external environment, other than the way I view things. Things that used to bother me no longer do. I am more creative and more confident. I see the difference in both my personal and professional life. My inner calm has a positive effect on everyone with whom I interact."

What is the distinction between patience (the subject of my prior book) and serenity? Since emotions are subjective experiences, each person will have their own distinctions. A general distinction is that patience is the ability to persevere, to repeat oneself, to wait calmly, to remain pleasant in the face of provocation, to endure distress or suffering. Impatience implies a lack of being able to cope well with an external source of frustration. Serenity is a peaceful inner state free from worry, frustration, and all forms of anxiety and stress. Some people are patient with others, but they themselves are not serene. Some people might be able to maintain serenity when they are by themselves, but they are not patient with other people. Both attributes are valuable. Once you have mastered one, you will find the other easier to attain.

In this as with the other books in this series, the stories are written in the first person even though they happened to various individuals. The stories have been written in a way that guarantees the privacy of the participants.

Be patient while you are mastering serenity. It is likely to take time. The second time you read this book each idea will be understood within the entire context of everything else that is written here. Questions that arise will be answered in different sections. Reread this book often. With each reading you will find yourself increasingly integrating the necessary attitudes and applying useful tools. Underline those ideas that you feel will be most beneficial. As you meet new challenges that arise, you will reach higher levels of serenity. Eventually serenity will become your spontaneous way of being.

I am grateful to the Almighty for all of His kindnesses. May this work enhance the lives of His children so they can better serve him.

I acknowledge my debt to all of my teachers — those who have taught me in person and those who have taught me through their writings. My father, of blessed memory, exemplified the human potential to be serene in the most challenging of situations. Rabbi Chaim Shmulevitz, the late Rosh HaYeshivah of Mirrer Yeshivah in Jerusalem, taught me the importance of attitude in creating our emotional lives.

I am extremely grateful to Rabbi Noach Weinberg, founder and director of Aish Hatorah for his teachings and for his making it possible for me to teach the concepts about which I write. I heartily thank Rabbi Kalman Packouz for his consistent encouragement. I am grateful for all the practical tools and techniques I gained from NLP (Neurolinguistic programming). The NLP model of accessing states gives us user-friendly tools to master positive inner resources.

I express my deep thank-you to Rabbi Meir Zlotowitz, Shmuel Blitz, and the entire ArtScroll staff for making this book possible.

1
Serenity Is up to You

The most important awareness for becoming serene is to realize that serenity is up to you. There are two myths that work against mastery of serenity. Right at the beginning it is imperative to clarify the truth.

Myth One: Believing that serenity is a gift that either you possess or do not possess. Some people are born with serenity and are fortunate. Someone who is not naturally serene has little hope of changing. This misconception is a major block.

Truth: Serenity is a learnable skill. Every normal human being has the ability to learn the basics. Your brain creates serenity or its opposite. If you frequently experience stress, anxiety, tension, frustration, anger, and other unresourceful states, these are created by the way that you use your brain. You have amazing potential to condition your brain so that you frequently create and access the state of serenity, along with other resourceful states such as joy, courage, and patience. With knowledge and persistence everyone has the potential to gain greater mastery over his emotional states.

Anyone who claims that we cannot is just saying that he has not yet learned this skill.

Myth Two: Believing that only when someone is in a perfectly peaceful environment can one maintain serenity.

Truth: Yes, it is much easier to be serene when you are in an ideal place with a peaceful atmosphere. Yes, it is much easier to be serene when all the people you interact with are rational, kind, and calm. Nevertheless, even when the external environment is far from being optimally fit for serenity, we have the ability to create an inner serenity and to resiliently bounce back when we temporarily lose it.

Step one for serenity mastery is to accept the concept that you personally can increase your level of serenity. Since serenity is within you and is created by your thoughts, you can learn the patterns that are conducive for serenity and eliminate limiting patterns.

While doing research for this book, I asked people who had not yet read it (of course), "What stops you from being serene?"

I received many answers. "I'm not serene because I wasn't born that way." "My family was dysfunctional." "My parents were high achievers and were always busy and in a rush." "My business is highly competitive." "I find school work difficult." "I have financial pressures." "I have so much to learn and I am constantly behind." "I have a busy schedule." "There are so many people who irritate and frus-

trate me." "Everyone in my profession experiences premature burnout."

No one answered, "I'm not serene because I haven't yet learned and mastered this skill." Since serenity is up to each individual this is the only accurate answer. When you put in the effort to master serenity, in retrospect you will be grateful that you did.

2

Make the Commitment

*B*e resolved with a strong sense of commitment to master serenity. The greater your realization of the magnitude of the benefits you will gain, the easier it will be to persevere even if the going gets rough.

Serenity promotes health and feelings of well-being. Your brain functions better when you are in a calm and relaxed state. Serenity increases your ability to think clearly, to concentrate for longer periods of time, to better understand what you read, to listen with greater focus, and to remember at optimal levels. You are more creative when you are in a serene state.

Serenity promotes peaceful and harmonious relationships with other people. We have often cited the verse, "As in water, face to face, so too is the heart of one person to another" (*Proverbs* 27:19). When you speak serenely to someone, the peaceful energy puts the other person in a better state, and usually that person will speak more pleasantly to you.

All the members of your family gain when you are serene. Serene children treat their parents with greater respect and serene parents influence their children to be more serene.

Serene employers and managers have a positive effect on their employees and those they supervise. A serene teacher has greater patience for students. A serene principal sets the tone for an entire school.

There really is no downside to being serene. When one needs to be more authoritative or to speak with greater intensity, a firmer approach will prove more effective for long-term results when one is usually serene than when it is presented with the aggressiveness of someone who is generally nervous or tough.

Awareness of what it is like not to be serene is a motivating factor for mastering serenity. Stress, tension, worries, fears, irritations, frustrations, resentment, anger, anxiety, etc., are the source of much human suffering. They create unpleasant feelings in the present, and are the cause of a long list of psychosomatic illnesses and pain. A person who suffers from stressful and unresourceful states will usually not treat other people with sufficient kindness, respect, love and compassion. It is difficult to empathize with others when one is preoccupied with one's own suffering. The root of many addictions such as overeating, smoking, drinking alcohol, etc., come from stress and anxiety. Serenity is the healthiest antidote.

A mind occupied with stressful thoughts and feelings will find it hard to concentrate during prayer and when studying. A mind weighed down with negativity is not free to focus on gratitude to the Creator for all His blessings and gifts.

As you review ideas that promote serenity, they will become an integral part of your automatic and spontaneous thinking. Your strong desire to become serene will eventually make this your reality.

I always thought that serenity was a quality that only a small minority could achieve. I never thought about attaining this trait since I didn't think I could do much about my usual stress, nervousness, tension, and self-consciousness.

What changed my mind was meeting one of the most serene individuals I had ever encountered. "You must have always been like this," I said to him.

"Not at all," he replied. "I was a high-strung child and a nervous young adult. But I read about the harm of excessive stress and this got me so nervous that I was committed to do whatever it took to master serenity. Although I did read as much as I could about the subject and spoke to various people, the number one thing that I consider to be at the root of my success was my total commitment to become a serene person. I had always admired people who had the elegance and nobility of serenity. I was intensely determined to gain this for myself."

3

This Moment

This moment is the only moment that exists for you right now. When you start reading this sentence, the previous sentence is already in the past and this is the sentence you are presently reading.

The next breath that you take, or that you are taking this second, is the only breath that exists for you in reality. Your last breath happened in the past, and your next breath did not yet happen.

When you speak to someone, each word you say is the only word that exists in the present. Your previous word happened in the past, and your next word will happen in the future.

The thought you are thinking in any given moment is the only thought that exists for you. Your last thought existed in the past and your next thought will be in the future. Since you are reading this, you cannot read these words and think other thoughts in the exact same second. You can switch back and forth quickly, but you can only do one at a time, either you read or you think.

Since you exist in only one moment at a time, to be serene you only need to be serene during that moment. You create serenity when you think serene thoughts and mentally picture serene scenes. You create serenity when you breathe slowly and deeply and relax your muscles. You create serenity when you vividly remember scenes of being serene. If you can access a serene state right now, it is obvious that you have the ability to do so this very moment. (If you cannot yet do this, read the entire book and then reread this section.) Thus, in any future moment that moment is the only moment that actually exists for you right then. So regardless of how you have been at any and all moments before and how you will be at any given moment later on, you only need to be serene this moment. Repeat these last four words: Be serene this moment.

Be serene this moment. Some moments will be more conducive for serenity and some moments will be more difficult. But whenever you repeat these words, your brain will be focused on serenity. The more frequently you repeat, "Be serene this moment," the more likely it is that this message will last for you even when you are not repeating these words.

The skill you need to master to be consistently serene is the ability to access serenity at will at the present moment. The rest of this book is commentary.

When I heard about the power of repeating, "Be serene this moment," I immediately realized that this is what I needed so greatly.. But how could I remember these words when I needed them the most? My refrigerator at home is a great place to post messages. But I often needed to remember this when I was faced with challenging situations out of the house. "I got it!" I said to myself. "I'll write it on my watchband. Every time I look at my watch, I'll have a reminder to be serene at that moment." It worked well for me and I'm certain it will work well for many others.

4

It's All in Your Thoughts

A tense life filled with stress or a vibrant life of serene energy are very different. Yet there is a single factor that they have in common. It is one's thoughts that create these emotional states.

What you focus on and how you evaluate and perceive events, situations, and occurrences are the deciding factors. Stress is not created by the specific events in one's life, but by the attitudes, perspectives, cognitions, frames, and evaluations that one has accepted as his subjective outlook. These are all thoughts.

There are many positive frames to choose from. Some are: "What is good about this?" "How can I grow from this?" "How can this help me develop my character?" "What could be beneficial about this in the long run?" "What could be humorous about this?" "How would someone experienced at reframing view this?" "What can I learn from this?" "How can I turn this around?"

Be aware which of your unique thought patterns create stress, tension, worry, frustration, and other unresourceful states. Then be aware of your personal thoughts and pictures with which you create your resourceful states such as serenity, joy, confidence, enthusiasm, courage, and compassion. This awareness will help you gain greater mastery. You will be able to consciously select the thoughts you prefer.

Master the ability not to allow stressful thoughts to settle in your consciousness. "It's just a thought," you can say to yourself. "And that is just a thought." "And this too is just a thought." Let counterproductive and unresourceful thoughts go. Focus on thoughts that are beneficial, helpful, resourceful, and a source of well-being. Focus on thoughts that create the states you want. Make a mental chain. Let unresourceful thoughts remind you to gently move on to positive, resourceful, empowering thoughts.

Find positive, resourceful, elevated, creative, spiritual attitudes and perspectives, for various situations, events, and occurrences. Masters of this skill think and analyze. If their original way of looking at something is not helpful, all the more so if it has proven counterproductive, they choose better attitudes, perspectives, frames, cognitions, outlooks, or evaluations. They realize that their initial response may not be the best and the wisest. So they pause to think for a moment and to find improved ways to view events and situations.

Is it easy or difficult to change the way you view something? It all depends, of course. The more enjoyable you find this, the easier it seems. And the more experience you have, the more proficient you will be at upgrading the way you view things, and the easier it will become. All of your thoughts about things were either learned from others or developed by yourself. You can learn new and better ways of thinking. You can develop outlooks that greatly enhance the quality of the way you feel, the way you talk, and the actions you take.

"Are thoughts really powerful enough to fight distressful emotions?" I asked.

With a smile I was told, "Your thoughts are what created your strong emotions in the first place. So, of course, thoughts that are real to you can change those emotions."

This seemed strange to me and my skepticism was obvious. My teacher continued, "When you consider something to be awful, or terrible, or a misfortune, or harmful, or dangerous, your nervous system reacts in ways that will motivate you to protect yourself. But when you realize what happened is for your benefit, it is a blessing in disguise, you will gain from what occurred. Due to this you have been saved from something much worse, you will become a better and stronger person, you will be able to help other people, your nervous system will react with relief, gratitude, and even joy. Think it over and you will certainly recall incidents that at first seemed to be problematic and then a change in perspective gave you an entirely different outlook."

Thinking it over, I recalled a number of examples. Since then I have been asking other people for their experiences. I find that the more instances I hear about, the easier it has become for me to change my own perspectives.

5

Reactions Toward Your Reactions

We always have reactions toward our reactions. That is, when we react with irritation, frustration, anger, worry, anxiety, guilt, fear, panic, etc., we have thoughts and feelings about those thoughts and feelings. The nature of these patterns will either increase stress and other distressful feelings, or will increase our feelings of well-being, serenity, and empowerment. (Neurosemantics calls these patterns meta-states, that is, states about our states.)

What is a stress-producing pattern? One feels upset about a trivial incident. Then one says something like, "I shouldn't have to experience this." Then one feels angry. Then one feels guilty about the anger. Then one feels sad about this. Then one tells oneself, "I keep feeling this way too often. I'll probably feel this way more often in the future." Then one feels worried about what this will mean in one's life. These patterns can go on and on, creating even worse feelings.

What is a resourceful pattern? You feel upset about a trivial incident. Then you say, "I can learn something valuable from this." Then you feel empowered since you visualize yourself implementing what you have learned. Then you feel calmer. Then you feel happy that you see yourself making progress. Then you tell yourself that you will be able to help others with what you now know. Then you feel the joy of being able to do many acts of kindness. Then you feel enthusiastic about your future. Then you feel relieved that you were able to take something that began as distressful and go with it to positive places. And this pattern goes on and on enhancing your life.

Regardless of how often you might have been having negative reactions toward your reactions, this very moment you can begin to create positive reactions. Even here some people react, "Oh no. You mean I've created a lot of my own suffering?" But this leads to more stress. A preferable pattern is to say to yourself, "I am joyous that I presently realize I create my thoughts and feelings (frames and states) and their chains. Now I'm committed to create a chain leading to ever-increasing serenity."

I've spent a lot of time and money trying to figure out why I am the way I am. While people gave me different insights, I still hadn't mastered joy and serenity. Then someone told me, "The root of your lack of joy and serenity is the pattern of your thoughts toward your feelings. Create a wiser, more resourceful pattern and you will experience new and better reactions. Your initial reaction is automatic, but where you go with it is up to you."

I was advised to write down my present patterns as they were happening. I did and this automatically motivated me to create better chains. Seeing them on paper made it totally clear that it would be stupid for me to keep creating negative, counterproductive chains.

6

Don't Buy Into the Unresourceful Attitudes of Others

*W*orking on developing the attitudes, perspectives, evaluations, frames and reframes that are conducive for serenity can take time and effort to master. Even after you put in the necessary energy, you must guard against acquiring others' unresourceful and counterproductive ways of looking at things. You would not pay money to buy these attitudes, so do not accept them even when they are given to you for free.

Being aware of the attitudes and outlooks that are life enhancing will make you more sensitive to what others say about situations and events. Some of the things you hear will further your quest for serenity. Other statements, opinions, and points of view are stress builders. Add the positive positions to your own mental library. And disregard those that are negative and counterproductive.

If you are like most people, you already have unresourceful perspectives and evaluations that you acquired from others. They may have become part of your own thinking and you may consider them to be the objective reality. As soon as you are aware of a needlessly negative perspective, ask yourself, "How can I view this in a wiser, better way?"

Some common negative attitudes are, "When this or that happens, you just have to become stressed out." "There's nothing one can do to change their feelings about this." "Your feelings are sacrosanct regardless of what those feelings are." "Your initial reaction is your true reality. Don't think you can fool yourself to try to change it." "Everyone I know views things this way so I must also be nervous and upset." These are subjective limiting frames. You never have to be stressed out unless you are physically exhausted. And even then you can feel calm about it. We have a tremendous ability to change our feelings about things. Feelings are all temporary based on how we presently perceive a situation. New and better perspectives and outlooks are always within our reach. The moment you change your thought, your nervous system changes how you feel. Life-enhancing thoughts create life-enhancing feelings. Even if this is only a subtle shift, you are moving in the right direction.

Recently a Cuban woman attempted to escape with her 6-year-old son from her husband. She perished in the effort but the boy was rescued and brought to the United States. A legal battle for custody of the boy erupted between his father who lived in Cuba and his mother's relatives in the United States. The courts ruled that he should return to his father in Cuba. A military operation was carried out to forcibly remove the boy from his mother's relatives.

Dr. Michael Hall, developer of "Neurosemantics" and "Metastates" and author ("Frame Games" and other NLP and Metastates books), was asked whether the boy would be traumatized by the experience. The gist of his answer was, "Even though many professional psychologists and psychiatrists have stated on the national media that the boy would certainly be traumatized, it really all depends. If he hears that he must be traumatized, it makes it more likely that he will be. But if he understands that he is greatly loved by many people and they all want what they think is best for him, he will have a totally different view of what he experienced. One's subjective frames create one's emotional reality."

7

Focus on Serenity

*W*hatever you focus on gets reinforced. When faced with a difficult, distressful, or challenging situation, it is easy to think of what you do not want.

"I don't want to be so nervous and anxious."

"I don't want to worry as much as I do."

"I don't want to be frustrated and upset so often."

"I don't want to be afraid of so many things."

"I don't want to feel such intense guilt for trivial oversights."

"I don't want to feel tense all of the time."

These are common ways of talking and they all increase stress. A person who says these sentences is thinking about being anxious, nervous, worried, fearful, frustrated, upset, or tense. This is the path of stress.

Focus on serenity. Use the word "serenity." Get in the habit of saying sentences like, "I would like to be more serene." "My goal is to master serenity." "I will be aware of what I can do to increase my serenity." "The way of serenity is going to be my way."

What if you are feeling anxious and tense? You can still say, "I'm not yet totally serene." At times the incongruity of this sentence will make you smile or laugh. This will be the beginning of your feeling calmer and more relaxed.

I was confronted by someone who challenged me, "You say that your thoughts create your emotions. How come my thoughts aren't creating the emotions I want?"

"What exactly are you saying to yourself?" I calmly asked.

"You know, thoughts about not being upset and nervous. I say, 'Stop being so worried. It's stupid to worry so much.'"

"Anything else?" I asked.

"Since this hasn't worked, I tell myself, 'That's enough time spent being stressed out.' And, 'You don't want to feel this way any longer.' It just doesn't work. I think that thoughts don't make a bit of a difference."

"I would like to make a suggestion that you experiment with the following sentences and see how they are helpful to you, 'Little by little, as I breathe slowly and deeply I am becoming more and more serene.' 'As I remember serene moments of the past, I am becoming more serene this moment.' And, 'Right now I am going to imagine what it would be like to be calm, peaceful, relaxed, and tranquil.' You can even try this right now." As the person repeated these sentences, it was obvious to both of us that he was becoming calmer.

8

It Adds Up

*E*very moment of serenity adds up. In the magnificent brain that the Creator gave you, you have every positive moment stored up. As we have written in previous books, every moment of joy, every moment of courage, every moment of serene empowerment is stored in your brain.

So whenever you are serene, you have a choice of two basic attitudes. One attitude is, "Isn't it awful that I'm not this way all the time!" Someone who thinks in this pattern botches up his serene moments.

A wiser path is to tell oneself, "Isn't it great that I feel serene now! This is presently being stored in my brain. It joins my other moments of serenity. The larger the library and storehouse of serenity in my brain, the easier it will be for me to access it at will.'"

In general, the good you do adds up. Cherish every precious action. The good feelings this engenders will increase the amount of good that you do in this world.

I was talking to someone about serenity and his first reaction was, "But I don't see how I can be serene all the time."

"I'm curious," I said to him. "Do you always have this pattern?"

"What pattern?" he asked.

"We are talking about increasing your level of serenity. It makes sense for you to initially focus on what you can do to be more serene. Why is your first response focused on not being able to do it all the time?"

"I never realized this was my pattern," he said. "It was just the first thought that came to my mind."

"If you make an effort to think about how and when you can apply positive ideas, you will gain in two ways. You will be thinking in the direction you want to go when you encounter valuable concepts and principles. And you will generally find yourself being more serene."

9

Talk to Yourself Serenely

*Y*ou are the person with whom you talk most often. To become a serene person, consistently talk to yourself serenely.

Become aware of the tone of your voice when you speak to yourself. This often is so automatic that many people never consider it an issue. But it can be a major factor in whether or not you are usually serene.

As an exercise, talk to yourself as you would if you were highly agitated, even panicky. Speak quickly and in a frazzled manner. Then speak very slowly and gently, softly and soothingly. Experience the difference between the two patterns.

One way to end up speaking serenely to yourself mentally is to practice speaking to yourself out loud when there is no one else around. By speaking out loud to yourself, you can gain a greater awareness of the tone you use. You can make this even more effective by making a tape recording of your voice as you speak to yourself. As you listen to this, ask yourself, "Did I sound serene?"

What you say as you speak to yourself is important. The question to ask yourself is, "Does what I generally say when I talk to myself make me more serene or less serene?"

If anyone with whom you speak frequently makes you feel more stress, more worried, more anxious, or more frustrated, you would strongly wish for this person to change his patterns. We can try to influence the way someone speaks to us, but we need that person's cooperation. When you try to change the way you speak to yourself, your own cooperation is all that you need. Theoretically this should be easier to accomplish.

Remember times and moments when you spoke to yourself in ways that created serenity. Let this serve as your model to continue doing so.

"I used to suffer a lot from anxiety," someone told me. "And I had to work hard to decrease it."

"What helped you the most?" I asked him.

"The awareness of how I personally caused myself much of the anxiety that I experienced," he replied. "It was suggested to me that I become aware of how I spoke to myself. At first I argued that I really didn't speak to myself. The idea of speaking to myself seemed strange. But I was told that everyone speaks to themselves whether they are aware of it or not.

"As an exercise, I wrote down my inner dialogues for thirty minutes each day for one entire month. It was difficult for

me to do this. But I kept it up. Just writing down what I was saying to myself automatically had an influence on what I was saying to myself. Now I recognize quickly when my self-talk creates needless anxiety and stress. I either change the subject or I change the way I speak."

10

Visualize Yourself Being Serene

*Y*our power of visualization is one of the most valuable gifts the Creator gave you. With your ability to imagine, you can develop every positive trait, state, pattern, habit, and way of being that you wish.

The downside of your ability to visualize is that this is how people create worry, needless fears, stress, anger, and other unresourceful states. They make mental pictures of distressful events happening, and these pictures, whether they are vivid or barely noticeable in one's consciousness, cause the body's muscles to respond with anxiety and stress. The good news is that if you can create any of these with your imagination, it means that your imagination is working. Now your task is to apply your imagination in ways that will enhance your life.

Mentally make a picture of yourself being serene. If you can do this easily, great. If you cannot yet do this easily, relax;

eventually you will be able to. Visualize a relaxing scene where you would certainly be able to feel calm. See details of the most peaceful place you could possibly imagine. Imagine what it would be like if all your work was finished and now you give yourself permission to relax. Imagine that all issues in your life are resolved. Imagine that you are totally safe and secure. Imagine that you have a complete feeling of well-being. See your face bearing the expression of a person who is totally calm and relaxed. See yourself talking and acting with complete serenity. See yourself sitting, standing, or walking the way a totally serene person would. Creating a serene state by visualizing yourself being serene even one time gives you confidence in your ability to create this mental picture again. If you can do it once, you will be able to do it many more times.

I don't make clear mental pictures. I've met many people who can mentally visualize with great clarity. But I'm not one of them. I used to think that visualization tools aren't for me. But then someone gave me reassurance that it's not necessary to see pictures clearly to utilize the power of imagination. Everyone has an imagination since everyone dreams when they sleep. It's just that some people are more aware of it than others. Even imagining that you are imagining a scene helps you benefit from the power of your brain to visualize positive attributes.

ll

On Being Serenely Unserene

$\mathcal{E}$xpecting to be unserene some of the time will make it easier for you to handle your unserene moments. And this will increase your moments of serenity.

At times we may be tired and worn out. At times we have much more to do than time allows. At times we are in an exceptionally great rush. At times we have to cope with real tragedies and heavy adversity. At times the unresourceful states of others might throw us off balance. At times memories of the past are weighing on us, and worries about the future creep in. The goal in these situations is to become serenely unserene.

How do you become serenely unserene? Let me ask you another question, "How does one become unserenely unserene?" The answer is that when we feel stressed, in emotional pain, overwhelmed, anxious, worried, upset, irritated, or frustrated we have an attitude about these feelings. When we are upset about being upset, worried about being worried, or fearful about being fearful, we add to our levels of stress and suffering. These are known as metastates, attitudes about our states. And realizing this gives us better options.

We have another choice. We can have a calm and accepting attitude toward our being in distressful states. The calmer we are about this, the lighter our burden.

Practice this right now. Put yourself in an unserene state. Then allow yourself to feel calm about being in this unserene state. Once you have done this one time experientially, you now have a resource for the future.

What if you cannot put yourself in an unserene state right now? Will you feel bad that you are not unserene? You may. But then you have the opportunity to be serene about this.

A person who heard me speak about being serenely unserene argued vehemently that he didn't think this was possible.

"How many people have to do this how many times to prove that it is potentially possible for others?" I asked.

Thinking it over he acknowledged that if one person has done this once it is humanly possible.

"But I don't think that I will ever be able to do this," he said.

"Can you remember a joyous moment in your life?" I asked him.

"Of course," he replied.

"Now remember another special moment in your life," I suggested after seeing him change his state to a more positive one. "Now another one. Then another one."

After he did this five times, I asked him, "How do you feel now?"

"Much better," he replied.

"Terrific, now you see how to go from unserene to more positive feelings. Do you recall how upset you were about the idea of being serenely unserene? You see that you can go from an unserene state to a much more resourceful state in just a few moments. You can do the same thing for yourself that I just did. So even if you are never able to be serenely unserene, you can still move from a state you don't want to a preferable one."

12

"This Too Will Upgrade My Serenity"

*T*wo types of situations will help you upgrade your serenity. There will be moments when you are serene. While building up your mastery of serenity, every time you feel serene, you can tell yourself, "This, too, will upgrade my serenity." Each time you repeat this sentence in a serene state, it gives more power to these words.

And there are the situations that challenge your ability to remain in a serene state. These are situations that take you off balance. You might become angry. You might experience high levels of stress or nervousness. You might become obsessive about something that worries you. Then you realize that you have not been serene and you mentally create a serene state. You might change your attitude. You might visualize serene scenes. You might mentally step back and just observe your thoughts and emotions from a serene place. Now you can say, "This, too, will upgrade my serenity."

Each time you resiliently bounce back and once again access serenity, you have yet another experience of upgrading your serenity. You are now more prepared to face similar challenges in the future. This is a very valuable perspective. Some people lose their serenity, and then feel awful that they did so. Then they feel discouraged. This is a needlessly counterproductive attitude. The positive awareness that each time you experience a challenge and manage to bounce back, this increases your level of serenity mastery, will not only prevent the negative effects of a negative loop, but will actually be creating a positive one.

It was suggested that I say, "This too will increase my serenity," whenever I could. But this didn't work for me. Every time I said this I had a feeling that I was fooling myself. I complained to the person who made the suggestion, and his response was empathetic. "Not everyone gains from the same approach," he said. "Perhaps you should skip this one. Maybe it's not for you."

"But how can you be certain it won't work for me?" I argued.

"I can't. But don't try it if you think it will have a negative effect."

What happened after that was that I no longer felt pressure to repeat this phrase. And then I said to myself, "What do I have to lose? Let me try it."

I figured that either it will help me and I will become more serene from saying this. Or else, I will stop saying this and will feel better for doing so. It was a real case of, "This too will upgrade my serenity."

13
The Nine Serenity-Creating Words

"**D**o you have a short statement that I can use as a tool to be serene when I have difficulty?"

Here is a transforming nine-word sentence:

"Be totally in the present with a calm attitude."

This does not sound very complex or complicated, does it? Can serenity be this simple? Yes, it can. We have complex and complicated patterns that take us away from serenity. But serenity itself is natural. Each of us was once an infant. Every infant is serene as long as he does not experience the pain of hunger or other distress. Every young child absorbed in playing with a toy is serene.

But what happens as we grow up? "The Almighty created humans simple, but they sought many intrigues" (*Ecclesiastes* 7:29). "The many intrigues," said Rabbi Samson Raphael Hirsch, "are the enemies of our happiness." Life has the potential for joy and serenity, but each person chooses what he will think about and how he will view things. Make wise choices. Think about all that you can be grateful for. Keep counting your blessings. Focus on the good that you can do. Master the skill of finding realistic positive frames and perspectives. As you do, what could potentially cause frustration and irritation will be sources of personal growth, creativity, and spiritual elevation. Each day you will have what to celebrate. Look for it and you will find it. Feel joy and a sense of accomplishment with each bit of progress.

Most of the thoughts that rob one of serenity have to do with being upset about the past and anxiety about the future. When you master the ability to live totally in the present and you are able to be calm about that present, you will have mastered serenity. One needs to plan ahead. This is one definition of a wise person. Do so serenely in the present.

In a classic Hebrew poem, Rabbi Eliyahu Eliezer Dessler has written:

"The past is only memories.

The future is but illusory hopes.

Focus on the present; for that is where your life really is.

And it consists entirely of challenges."

(Michtav MeiEliyahu, vol. 3, p. 306)

Rabbi Mordechai of Lechovitz related: "From the day I reached a level of understanding, I haven't worried a single time about what will be in a single hour."

A major tool for being in the present mentally is to focus on your breathing. You are breathing right now. Be totally present as you slowly inhale and exhale. If your mind wanders, calmly bring it back. Keep practicing this. Wouldn't it be wonderful if you were able to be calm in the present every time you breathe? This is a worthwhile goal toward which to strive.

Another tool for being in the present is to listen to those who are speaking with a total sense of being there. Listen to understand. Observe the choice of words and what they mean to the speaker. Listen calmly. Every experience of listening is the experience of entering someone's world. At times you will learn new things. At other times you will be doing a great act of kindness. At all times you will be able to use this as an exercise of being totally in the present. It can help to focus on the speaker's lips; this is a tool for concentration.

The skill of mastering serenity is being able to be calm in the present. You never have to deal with the future in the future. Even in the future, you will only have to cope with the present. So being calm in the present is all that you need to master. And since you are always in the present, you will have many opportunities to practice being calm in the present. You can even practice right now.

I was facing too many challenges all at once. My financial situation was shaky. Some projects I was working on weren't going as well as I had hoped. A close relative was in the hospital. A few members of my family were on edge and interacting with them was getting difficult. I sought advice and it was suggested that I write down the words, "Be totally in the present with a calm attitude." Just hearing these words immediately had a calming effect on me. I wrote them down in a place where I would easily see them. I repeated them to myself over and over again. They worked for me like magic.

14

Fifteen Seconds Ago

or those who have mastered serenity, fifteen seconds ago is ancient history. They realize that once something is over, it is over regardless of whether it has been over for many years or for a relatively short time. It is understandable that it can take different people varying amounts of time until they are able to let things go. But the goal should be to let go of what is over and done with. In truth, it is gone whether or not you let it. It is just a question of the degree of emotional mastery that you will have. Regardless of where you are at this moment, you can always improve on your ability to let things go as soon as they are gone.

• If someone insulted a master of serenity one minute ago, it is now over. Why needlessly rerun the insult in one's brain? You do not have to keep picturing it and you do not have to keep repeating the insult to yourself. You do not even need to keep repeating how much you did not like it.

• If you missed an opportunity, even if this was a major one that will not repeat itself, focus on new opportunities.

"But this opportunity won't come back," some people keep telling themselves. That is precisely the reason why it is wise to look for new opportunities. Once an opportunity has passed, it is gone. Do not waste time and energy repeating to yourself how awful it is that you lost out on this opportunity. View that opportunity as ancient history. Focus now on opportunities from which you can presently gain. View the present as an opportunity to build up your ability to master resourceful states even when this is challenging.

- If someone refused to do you a favor when you were a young child, you will probably find it easier to let it go than if someone refused to do you a favor a few minutes ago. The faster you let these sorts of things go, the more serene you will be. If you keep aggravating and frustrating yourself over what already happened, you can be just as upset with yourself as with anyone else. You personally are robbing yourself of having serenity. But ideally do not be upset even with yourself. This is not beneficial. Rather, view your being upset about the refusal of someone to do you a favor as ancient history, and be grateful that now you have a greater ability to let it go.

- If you got into an argument with someone, once the argument stops, consider it over and done with. Don't keep replaying it in your mind. If you do, you will be allowing your brain to focus on that and not on gratitude and serenity.

- If you made a mistake, acknowledge it. Correct what can be corrected. Make amends. Learn from it. Grow from it. But in the present, it is ancient history. Do not needlessly obsess on it in counterproductive ways. Do not waste your present moments when you can utilize them more wisely.

A word of caution: If someone is hurt or upset due to something you have said or done, you may need to apologize more than once. If that person is in distress, do what you can to alleviate it. Do not callously tell someone who is in pain, "That's history already." To you it may be history, but to that person it is still the present. Be sensitive to that.

I was told about an issue that bothered me, "Put it behind you."

But I couldn't. The emotional distress was too strong. I spoke to someone about it, and he explained the concept of time-lines (developed by neurolinguistic programming).

"Think about something that happened recently," he said. "Notice how your mind represents this. Then think about something that happened long ago and your inner feelings are that this is something that happened so far in the past that it no longer bothers you at all. That is your brain's personal way of differentiating between the two incidents.

"Now take something that actually happened recently and mentally move it back the same way you would if it were to have happened a very long time ago. When you do this, you'll see that it will be much easier for you to let go of the emotional distress of what has already happened."

15

"I Have So Much to Do"

"*How can I be serene? I have so much to do.*"

"*Everyone I know gets stressed out when there are a lot of things to take care of.*"

"*My 'to do' lists keep growing and the longer they are the more anxious I become.*"

If you have a lot to do, that is just great. It means you are alive and are capable of doing things. The way to accomplish in a calm fashion is to be efficiently organized. The more organized you are, the more you will be able to accomplish serenely. You will see what is reasonable to expect of yourself and what not.

If you have a lot to do, you will have an equal amount to do whether you are stressed or serene, right? The major difference is that if you are serene, you will probably be able to accomplish more with greater speed in a calm state.

When you are serene, you think with greater clarity. You can decide which task takes priority. You can figure out ways to delegate some of the jobs on your "to do" or "action" list.

What is the distinction between times you become stressed or overwhelmed when you have a lot to do and times you remain calm? The difference is essentially how you view the situation and how you talk to yourself.

The path of stress is to talk to yourself in a stressful manner. Your inner tone of voice is too fast, even frantic. The items are jumbled in your mind. You repeat to yourself, "I have too much to do. I can't manage. I'll never be able to do it all."

The path of serenity is to make a mental queue. List what you have to do one by one. Keep a written list and mark off priorities. Knowing that you will take care of the main objectives, you can be calmer about the exact details. You soothingly say to yourself, "I'm doing as much as I can. Keeping cool, calm, and collected will enable me to accomplish at my optimal level."

It might be worthwhile to consult an expert on organization for suggestions on how to be even more efficient.

Finally, even if you lack organizational skills, it is preferable to remain calm and disorganized rather than anxiety ridden and disorganized. It is a lot healthier and there is a better chance that you will eventually learn the necessary skills to get the most done in the least amount of time.

Be aware of what is really important for you to do in all areas of your life. Keep your main focus on accomplishing what is most valuable. Idealistic people always have much more they would like to accomplish than is actually possible. This is admirable and praiseworthy. Serene idealistic people are those who accept this reality calmly.

I became totally overwhelmed whenever I had a lot to do. I did function, but I had panicky feelings that slowed me down.

"This is just my basic personality," I repeated frequently. "I'm not an organized person."

A discussion with someone who had a large family and was always organized changed my position.

"You probably have a different personality than I do," I said.

"No, I don't. It's just that I learned how to be organized. This is a skill you too can learn. Read books on the subject; each one will give you several practical tips. Attend classes. If need be, take some lessons on a one-to-one basis which are geared to you personally."

Following this advice, I learned that what I was lacking was the knowledge of how to be organized. Accessing it and following it enabled me to be organized. And then others probably perceived me as having an organized personality.

16

You Are Valuable

O ne's sense of self-worth can either be a source of positive feelings or of distress. Having a deep realization of your intrinsic value protects you from the need to prove to anyone else that you are an important person. Knowing your unlimited value, you are free from the stress experienced by those who lack this understanding.

The Torah view of humans is that we are all created in the image of the Creator. Realizing that "each person is obligated to say, 'The universe was created for me,'" (*Talmud, Sanhedrin* 37a) gives you more value than any possible mortal accomplishment. Viewing yourself as a child of the Creator and Sustainer of the universe adds greatly to your sense of personal value. Of course, you want to accomplish and to develop your character. But this is adding another layer onto the foundation of your innate value and worth. You already have immense importance right from the start.

Self-image is how you view yourself. In reality it is easy to view yourself the way others view you. But ultimately it is you who selects which view you will accept. Some people access the view of negative individuals and make it their own. This is not a wise choice. Select the views of those who realize you are created in the Almighty's image, you are a child of the Creator, and the world was created for you. Why settle for anything less? And make certain that the one individual whose opinion makes the most difference in your life views you in this way. That person is you.

Feelings of self-importance that come from arrogance and conceit are counterproductive. These feelings are fragile and vulnerable. They make you dependent on external factors over which you do not have control. They create conflict with others. They could even make you slightly obnoxious. Those with a true sense of innate self-worth have the courage to be humble and modest. They do not feel a need to prove their worth. They do not have a need to boast or show off. Their sense of value is solid and secure.

"How can I feel good about myself?" the young man asked. "I have many faults. I haven't accomplished very much. So many others are better than me and have accomplished more than I ever will."

"First of all, your value isn't up to you. Your Creator gave you value whether you like it or not," the Rabbi told him. "You can choose to deny your value. But if you do it will be

a detrimental decision. Secondly, by recognizing your precious value, you will become a better person and will accomplish more. You have everything to gain and nothing to lose. Why live in the darkness of denial of your value when you can live in the light of knowing who you really are." The young man's face lit up.

17

Gratitude: An Ingredient for Serenity

*L*ack of gratitude is at the root of discontent. In order to be consistently serene, we must master the attribute of being grateful to the Creator for all of his gifts. As the Torah (*Deuteronomy* 26:11) states, "Rejoice with all the good the Almighty has given you." This does not negate our wanting more. But it does mean that we have a constant feeling of gratitude since as long as we are alive, we always have a list of things for which to be grateful.

As the Sages stated in the often-quoted adage, "Whoever has 100 wants 200. And whoever has 200 wants 400." It is human nature to never be totally satisfied with what we have. We always want more. This has a major spiritual benefit in that we always want to grow more in important areas when we personally consider them important to us. No amount of good deeds is ever sufficient. At the same time, in order to live a top-quality life, we need to appreciate and be grateful for what we already have.

The question to keep asking yourself is, "What five things am I grateful for right now?" Especially remember to ask yourself this as soon as you realize that you are feeling bad about not having all that you would wish to have. We never have all that we would wish. So the only way to live a joyous, serene life is to be grateful for what you do have even though you would really want more.

"As a child I was repeatedly told that I was spoiled," my sick friend told me. "I do remember that I was never satisfied for long with anything I received. I was happy with a new toy or game for a day or two. But shortly afterwards I wanted new toys and games. Being repeatedly told that I was spoiled only succeeded in giving me a negative self-image.

"As I became older it was important for me to always have enough money to buy what I wanted. I didn't demand the fanciest house and the most expensive clothing, but I did feel that I couldn't be happy unless I had the latest gadgets and appliances. Even when I could afford new things, I realized that it wasn't practical for me to buy every upgraded model. So hardly anything satisfied me for long.

"Now that I am ill, my attitude has changed. I don't know how long I will live. But I am dedicated to utilize all the time I have left to its fullest. I am now grateful for every morsel of food that I can eat. I am grateful for so many simple things that I used to take for granted. Every once in a *while, I feel awful for all the lost time. But I realize that this, too, is counterproductive thinking. I tell everyone who visits me how important it is to enjoy and appreciate what you have. It gives me strength to think that I am enriching the lives of others by encouraging them to learn from my mistakes."*

18

Meaningful Goals

We humans have a firm need for life to have meaning. Even if all of one's physical needs are met in a way that one has absolutely nothing about which to complain, life can be boring and meaningless. We need to be involved in matters that give us a strong sense of purpose. Conversely, even if one is in situations and circumstances that are highly challenging, if one has a strong sense of purpose, he will be able to cope and handle the challenges with inner feelings of well-being.

Goals themselves can be a source of stress and tension. We can feel pressure to reach our goals and feel that we are far behind in our quest. We can be anxious that we may never reach the goals we set for ourselves. We worry about how awful we would feel if we fail to accomplish as much as we would like. We can be envious of the accomplishments of others. Those who have not set goals might not focus on the success of others in reaching their goals. But those who are goal oriented may feel bad that others have achieved goals that they themselves could never reach.

Be serene about setting and reaching goals. If a goal is truly out of your reach, that goal is not yours. No matter how many goals one has reached, potential goals exist that one will not reach. There are goals of knowledge and creativity. There are goals of spiritual elevation. There are goals of character perfection. There are goals of kindness. There are goals of world peace, curing diseases, eliminating hunger and homelessness, solving the problems caused by alcohol and drugs, making certain that everyone drives carefully and crosses streets carefully thereby preventing car accidents that maim and kill. In reality we can each do only a small percent of what needs to be done.

The way to live life with positive emotional states is to have a sense of humility about what we are doing and what we can do. At the same time we should aim high. As my teacher Rabbi Gavriel Ginsburg frequently said, "When you reach for the stars, you may not catch any – but at the very least, you won't get your hands full of mud." Learning what we can learn is a meaningful goal. Improving our character even though we are far from perfection is a meaningful goal. Helping the people we can help is a meaningful goal. Raising one's family with love and instilling lofty values is a meaningful goal. Heeding one's words so as not to cause harm and pain and teaching this concept by example is a meaningful goal. Achieving these goals is time consuming but that is what time is intended for. Accomplishing what we can accomplish with joy and serenity is the way to live a life which is emotionally healthy.

I come from a family of high achievers. I live far from my extended family and find meaning in my daily life. But when I visit my family, I feel highly stressed. They all seem to be involved in matters that are more important than what I am doing with my life. This makes me sad on a deep level. I spoke to my Rabbi about this. He pointed out that what I was doing in my life was more meaningful than I gave myself credit for. In spiritual matters and personal growth, I was accomplishing in ways that were unique to me. In addition, it is important to be aware that we each have different missions in this world. My task was to achieve my goals — not the goals intended for someone else. For example, someone born with a handicap might not objectively accomplish as much as someone without that handicap. But by utilizing one's time and energy, one subjectively has accomplished more and that is what really counts in the long run when our entire life is taken into consideration. I was told to keep setting reachable goals and to feel profound pleasure and joy in the daily actions I took to reach my goals. Each action might seem tiny but I was building my character and I was having a positive effect on the lives of others. I should keep my eyes open to find opportunities that I might not have noticed or been aware of if I hadn't been searching. This discussion had a powerful effect on my emotional states.

19

Serene Empowerment

*P*art of being serene is to remain in a serene state even when you need to speak and act with empowerment. Being serenely empowered means that you say what you need to say and do what you need to do while you are inwardly feeling calm and relaxed.

Being serenely empowered is an antidote to anger. You do not need to experience anger to express your thoughts, feelings, wants, or wishes. Those who are able to be in a state of serene empowerment will have all the advantages of being serene and of being empowered.

Think of situations in which serene empowerment would be beneficial for you. These may be situations where you have lacked a sense of empowerment in the past. Or these may be situations where you have spoken up or taken action but have been overly nervous, upset, angry, or explosive. If you would have been calm and clear thinking you would likewise have said or done something, but it would have been a wiser and more effective act.

Mentally practice being serenely empowered. Visualize specific situations. You may find it beneficial to practice this while looking in a mirror. A mirror is an amazing feedback machine. Since mirrors are readily available it is easy to overlook how powerful practicing in front of a mirror can be.

I hate getting into arguments or quarrels. Frequently I will let things go and avoid situations that could become confrontational. When something gets me very angry, I will scream or shout. But afterwards I feel bad, even becoming obsessive, about how wrong it was of me to react with anger.

I've thought about how I would like to be. But when I see people who are very assertive, I feel that they are too aggressive for me. Finally I found a role model. I was in the presence of someone who was calmly assertive whenever he had a need to speak up. After hearing the term "serene empowerment," I realized that this is his pattern. I mentally practiced this and then put it into action. It was a great relief for me to see that I didn't have to choose to be either passive or aggressive. Serene empowerment is what I had been seeking.

20

Serene Zerizus

*I*t is easiest to be serene when one is relaxing in a peaceful garden and does not have any responsibility. To live an active life of accomplishment is more difficult. For this we need to develop the character trait of *zerizus* together with serenity.

What is *zerizus*? It is being alert which enables you to take action with appropriate speed. *Zerizus* is the opposite of laziness and procrastination. Two people may have similar levels of intelligence, skills, and talents. Yet the one who has a much higher degree of *zerizus* will accomplish much more.

Some people may think that if someone is always doing things quickly, he will seem frazzled and hyper. But the goal to strive for is to have serene *zerizus*. In the words of Rabbi Noach Weinberg, "Make haste slowly." That is, be serene even while you are utilizing your energy to act and accomplish.

I used to regard those who were calm and relaxed as lazy.
As a general rule, they didn't seem to accomplish as much

as those who were always in a rush. I used to admire people who had a frantic air about them. They seemed tense but this was the price they were willing to pay for getting things done.

Someone pointed out that a particular acquaintance was highly efficient and effective. Yet he always seemed as if he had all the time in the world. He never wasted time, but he didn't give you the feeling that he was trying to rush you.

Since then I consider this person as my role model for serene zerizus. This has been very helpful in increasing the number of things I am able to take care of in shorter amounts of time. And the added benefit is that my increased serenity has given me more energy than I ever had before.

21

Serene Time Management

*S*erene time management is a balance between two extremes. Some people are overly lax about time. They tend to come late even for important meetings. Others are overly concerned about being on time. They dread being late for anything and this creates heightened levels of tension whenever they must be on time or complete a task by a specific deadline. Those who are lax about being on time create stress for others. Those who are overly concerned about being exactly on time often create stress for themselves when circumstances beyond their control prevent them from being on time.

The ideal to strive for is to remain serene while you consider it important to be on time and to finish tasks and projects by the time that you or others designate for them. Develop a sensible perspective. Differentiate between situations when being on time is a high priority and when it does not really make a major difference.

It was always important for me to be on time. People joked about how they could set their clocks by my actions since they knew that I was certain to keep to a schedule. There were many advantages to this pattern. But the downside was that I was under pressure. The tension I experienced frequently led to my becoming angry at family members for being late. I would never enjoy going to any gathering since I was under a lot of tension while I got ready to go.

After an especially unpleasant interaction with some family members who were the cause of my being late when I wanted to be on time, I resolved to adopt a lighter attitude toward time. While it was still important to me to be on time, I had a more balanced perspective. I would weigh the matter objectively to see if it was really that necessary for me to be on time in each situation. Even when being on time was important, I tried not to look at being late as a major tragedy. By being more serene myself, I was able to rush other people much more gently. This motivated them to hurry so I could be on time. My new approach didn't cause resentment, so by being more at ease about being on time, I was on time more often when others were involved than I used to be.

22

Interviewing Calm People

*W*ould you like to become an expert on how to be calm in all sorts of challenging situations? Do not just rely on your own ingenuity. Keep asking people who appear to be calm, "Would you mind if I ask you how you are able to be so calm?"

My experience is that most people will happily share their thoughts on the subject with you. They will react positively to the fact that you observed that they are calm. Some might tell you that inwardly they are not as calm as they might seem on the outside. You will gain from this by realizing that others also experience challenges to their serenity. "When many suffer, it is half of a consolation." It enables us to say to ourselves, "I see that many others react the way I do."

Some people may provide details about how they manage that are not applicable to your situation. They may be able to afford hired help. They may have family members to help out. They may not have to take care of as many things as you do. This, too, is helpful. You thought you were in the same situation as they are and you are finding it rougher than them. Now you realize that the reason they are able to remain calm is that their situation is different than yours.

And then you will hear attitudes, outlooks, and perspectives that you can adopt as your own. You may learn ways of looking at things that you did not think of before. You might have been aware of these same ideas and now that you have role models for them it will make it easier for you to emulate their example. You may learn of new tools and techniques, or how to actually use those that you have read about but did not yet apply.

When you become calm and serene, others may ask you how you do it. Then you will have opportunities to do acts of kindness for them which they will then be able to pass on to others.

It was suggested that I ask seemingly calm people how they remain calm. The very thought of asking others such a personal question made me nervous. "What if they get angry at me for asking? What if they answer, but inside they feel something must be wrong with me for asking them this question? What if they refuse to answer me?"

"So you aren't calm about asking this question?" I was asked.

"That's an understatement," I replied.

"I personally enjoy asking this question, ask me how I do it," I was told.

"O.k., how do you do it?" I asked.

"Did you feel calm about asking me this question?"

"Sure."

"See you know how to do it."

"But I knew that you wouldn't mind if I asked you since you asked me to," I argued.

"Since you don't mind asking this question to people who don't mind, just ask it to people you think will be willing to answer you."

I did and I saw that the people I asked were happy to share their approaches. I began to realize that people who are calm will also be calm about being asked questions about how they stay calm.

23

The Serenity Question

There is an effective question you can ask yourself that will easily help you access serenity. Try this a number of times and see how you can utilize its power.

The question to ask yourself is, "If I were serene right now, what would I be like – specifically?" Repeat this a number of times to make this question automatic.

If you were serene right now, how would you be breathing? As you breathe the way you would if you were serene, you will become more serene.

If you were serene right now, how would your muscles be? Mentally scan your entire muscle system and allow your muscles to be the way they would be if you were serene.

If you were serene right now, what would you be thinking? What would you be saying to yourself and in what tone of voice? Say them now.

What mental pictures would you be seeing if you were serene right now? See them now.

When you talk to another person or to a group of people, how would you talk if you were totally serene?

Many people have found this question helpful. If you also do, it would be worthwhile to keep this question in a place where you will frequently see it. After a while, such messages often become so familiar that you cease to notice them. If this happens, remove the question for a few days and then replace it so it stays fresh in your mind.

24
Mentally Prepare for Challenges

*T*he more mentally prepared you are for challenges to your being in a serene state, the greater your ability to maintain this state. Some people are able to put themselves in a serene state when it is quiet all around and no one is there to create stress. This is definitely an achievement. For it is easy to create inner stress even when no one else is around. But the goal to strive for is to be able to remain in a serene state even when other people say and do things that could potentially cause distress.

How do you prepare yourself mentally? Allow yourself to enter a serene state. Mentally visualize a serene place. Talk to yourself serenely. Remember serene moments. Close your eyes and with your eyes looking slightly upwards, see yourself being serene. Breathe serenely. Imagine what it would feel like if you were absolutely serene right now. When you are serene, make a unique hand motion or finger signal that your brain will associate with this state (an "anchor" in NLP, Neurolinguistic-programming terminology). As you feel serene, soothingly repeat the word "serene."

Then mentally visualize people saying things to you that might previously have caused you irritation, frustration, anger, and any other form of stress. Maintain your serene state regardless of what you imagine they say. As you successfully do this, intensify the potential negativity. Think of words that have bothered you in the past; imagine them being said to you right now. Maintain your serene state. If you begin to access a distressful state, stay calm about this. Reread the previous paragraph. Take pleasure in the entire process of expanding your brain and your ability to maintain serenity.

In *Anger: The Inner Teacher* (pages 363-76) there is a list of over three hundred challenging situations. You may find it helpful to put yourself in a serene state and read the list visualizing each scene as you maintain a serene state throughout the exercise. This mentally prepares you for the real thing.

The goal is to practice remaining serene regardless of what anyone says. Knowing that you can do this in your imagination will free you from worrying about what anyone may say in the future. And if anyone actually does say something insulting or anger provoking, you will be able to stay serene since you have already practiced this in advance.

If you do lose your serenity in an actual situation in the future, relax. This just represents feedback which tells you that you need additional practice. With sufficient practice, you will become proficient.

Someone told me that twenty years before, he saw a master in a highly specialized form of martial arts practicing his exercises. He only saw him once, but the memory came back when he wanted to master serenity. The man stood in the middle of a circle and all around him other practitioners shouted and screamed at him at the top of their lungs. They did everything they could to make him flinch. The goal was for him to stay so centered that nothing anyone said or did would get him off balance. He had just realized that he could mentally do this to practice maintaining serenity.

25
Being Real With Your Feelings

*T*hinking about serenity and realizing its great value, we would love to be serene all the time. But this is not possible in the world in which we live. In the totality of our lives we will experience a wide range of human emotions, not all of them the ones we would choose for ourselves if we could have total control over our feelings. So now we have a choice: We can acknowledge our emotional reality at any given moment and from there work our way to true serenity. Or we can deny our true feelings. We may deny our insecurities, anxieties, worries, frustrations, disappointments, etc., and think that because we want to be serene, these feelings do not exist. Let us state clearly: Only by being in touch with your feelings will you be able to truly experience serenity.

Being aware of your feelings does not mean that you should act out on your anger, your fears, your worries, and your insecurities. You want to be the master of what you say and do even when your present emotional states are not conducive to speaking and acting at your best.

Being real does mean that you are aware of your actual thoughts and feelings at a given moment. And from that place, you access the thoughts and feelings that you would prefer.

All of your anger, your fears, your worries, your anxieties, and your stress come from your focus and your perspectives. You have the ability to shift your focus to thoughts and places where you will be calmer, more relaxed, more in control, and more serene. You have the ability to change your perspectives. You can find attitudes, frames, and ways of looking at things that will immediately change your feelings. Your first reaction may be that a minor difficulty is "awful" and "terrible." Then you step back and realize that this is a "challenge" and an "adventure." You think a little more and realize that this is "an opportunity" and "a great benefit." Your real feelings will now change. You were able to change them because you knew what they were and how you caused them. Then you were able to shift to different feelings.

Your feelings are all temporary. Gaining expertise in accessing serenity by reviewing the ideas in this book and applying the tools will make it easier for you to acknowledge whatever state you are in at a given moment. When you are in an unresourceful state, you can calmly and objectively say to yourself, "I am in an unresourceful state right now. Let me think of ways to access a more resourceful state." The more frequently you access serene states, joyous states, empowered states, humorous states, enthusiastic states, and creative states, the more likely these will be your real, spontaneous, and automatic feelings. This takes practice. Enjoy the entire process.

A highly emotional artist told me, "I used to think that people who reacted with more positive feelings than I did in difficult situations were just faking. 'They couldn't be taking this so positively,' I thought to myself. At times I acted as if I felt better than I actually did. I didn't want others to know how vulnerable I was. I wanted to be calm and relaxed as a general way of being. But my reality was that I was intense and high strung. Working on serenity made me tense. I felt that this was preventing me from being myself even though I didn't like the way I was.

"After much time and effort thinking about serenity and discussing this with others, I realized that I mistakenly thought that my initial reactions were my identity. I grew up in an emotionally tumultuous house, and serenity wasn't in our vocabulary. As I developed attitudes and tools conducive to serenity, I realized that my real feelings were highly fluid. I developed the habit of using the word 'state' for my feelings. I kept a list of my favorite states and accessed them frequently. I knew that I would frequently be in nonserene states. I take this more lightly than I used to, and this makes it easier for me to shift my real feelings from distressful ones to healthy and enjoyable ones."

26

Don't Try Too Hard

*T*rying too hard to maintain serenity will create more stress than if one were not working on becoming serene. Be calm and patient about becoming serene. Let the process take as long as it takes. Do not attempt to rush it.

Whenever you try too hard to do anything, you will experience stress. With other goals, you may still reach your goal even though you are creating needless stress for yourself. But when you try to master serenity, creating stress will prevent you from achieving your goal.

You may attempt to be serene in your interactions with someone and that person continually does or says things that cause you to become upset or angry. It is easy to become even angrier if you feel that this person is the cause preventing you from being serene. Not only will you be angry at him for the original reason, now your anger will be increased because he is not enabling you to be serene.

While you are correct in wanting to be serene and in considering this goal as very important to attain, you still need to take the process as lightly as you can. "How can I take it lightly when I realize how important it is to be serene?" Resolving this dilemma is exactly what you need to do to consistently work on mastering serenity and at the same time maintaining serenity while you do so.

This is similar to taking an important test. You want to do well. But if you are excessively nervous, that nervousness can prevent you from thinking as clearly as you would if you were calm. Here, too, one needs to master a balance. You need to consider the test as important enough to spend time studying the material. And at the same time you need to be relaxed when you take the test so your brain will function at its optimal level.

If you find that you are trying too hard to become serene, tell yourself to calm down. Some people find that this is more effective when they have permission to take it easy. If this applies to you, then take this paragraph as your personalized permission to go easier on yourself.

"I have been told that being serene is very important for me. But the more I try, the worse I feel. Whenever I put in the effort to become more serene, I am more stressed out than before I tried," the young man complained.

"What are you telling yourself when you try?" he was asked.

"I don't know," he honestly replied.

"The next few times you try to become serene, be more aware of what you are telling yourself about what you are

doing," he was told. "Once you know how you are creating this stress, you will see what thoughts you need to change to ensure success."

By paying careful attention to his self-talk he realized that both his tone of voice and the content of what he was telling himself needed to be changed. He had repeated to himself, "It's really awful that you are trying so hard and you are still stressed out. The more you try, the more you are proving to yourself that you will never really be serene. You are failing at this, just as you've failed at many other things."

He was relieved to find this out about his pattern of self-talk. Now he was on his way to change the script. He followed the suggestion that he should say to himself, "Each time you work on serenity, you gain more self-knowledge. You learn what works for you and what doesn't. You also learn what you need to do to modify the approaches you try. You deserve credit for the effort you are making." And this was conducive for increasing his serenity even before he totally succeeded.

27

Utilize the Power of Autosuggestion

*A*utosuggestion is when you repeat statements to yourself in order to integrate and internalize valuable messages. This has proven itself to be a powerful tool when used properly.

Right at the outset it is important to know that if someone feels certain that autosuggestion will not work for him, he is both right and wrong. Telling oneself that autosuggestion will not work will make only one autosuggestion work. And that is the suggestion that any other suggestion besides this one will not work. This one will work powerfully and it will block out the skill of giving oneself more beneficial autosuggestions.

Autosuggestions must be worded positively. Repeat what you do want (not what you do not want). Therefore you say to yourself, "I am becoming more and more serene each and every day." Or even, "I am becoming more and more serene with each step that I take," when you are walking. You are not necessarily making a statement of present fact. You are telling your brain the messages that you want the brain to make your reality.

When you repeat to yourself statements such as, "I am becoming more and more serene," speak to yourself in a calm, soothing voice. Some people repeat this a few times in a fast, skeptical voice and of course it does not work. Any tool — regardless of how potentially powerful — that one uses not in accordance with the operating instructions of that tool will not work. Autosuggestion fits into this category. Since using positive words and speaking calmly are fairly simple techniques, it makes sense to try it out.

Believe that you will be able to give yourself suggestions to create a greater level of serenity. If you have benefited from autosuggestion in other ways, it will be easier for you to believe that it will work for you with serenity. If at the present serenity is too much of a challenge, utilize autosuggestion for confidence and courage ("I am feeling more and more confident." "I am increasing my level of courage with every breath I take.") or with joy ("I am more and more joyous each and every day."). When you see that you are becoming more confident, more courageous, and more joyous, you will know with greater clarity that you will also become more serene.

I am highly suggestible and I have used autosuggestion many times. That is, I experience the emotional quality of words very easily. This has been a strength for me and has also caused me pain, since words effect me strongly. I am working on making myself less vulnerable by learning to close down my openness to suggestions when they create unresourceful states. One of my biggest challenges in this area was to overcome the lack of belief in autosuggestions by others. Some of these individuals have very strong personalities. When they would say, "It's a bunch of nonsense to believe that words can affect you so strongly," I was open to their suggestions and questioned my ability to condition myself with autosuggestion. When I finally realized that this itself was a product of my being open to suggestion, I was totally determined that I would be the one to decide which suggestions I would allow my brain to accept. I've even come up with an autosuggestion, "The more anyone challenges my ability to give myself autosuggestions, the more powerful my ability will become." Now I appreciate these challenges; they strengthen me.

28

Create a Mental Haven

*W*hen we travel to locations noted for their tranquil settings, we become calm and relaxed. The scenery, the weather, and everything about those areas enable us to let go of all tension and stress. Many wish they could stay far longer than circumstances allow.

Actually, however, it is not the place that enables one to feel this inner peace. It is one's mind which accomplishes this. When the setting is just right, our minds let go of all the factors that prevent us from feeling serene. And serenity is what we experience.

There is a downside to the need to go away in order to achieve serenity. We cannot always get away from our busy schedules. We have responsibilities and obligations. We may have financial constraints that do not allow us to travel or limit how long our vacation will last. And the reality is that no place on this planet will be totally perfect. Factors can always arise to make a potentially great vacation less than memorable.

The good news is that your mind has the ability to create a serene personal haven. The magical place you can visualize is truly perfect. The spectacular gardens, the gentle background music, the soothing waves of the ocean, the magnificent mountains, your special mosaic of woodlands and grasslands, beautiful birds flying gracefully overhead, the total tranquility are all in your personal power. When you mentally come to your personal haven, you immediately feel all tension and stress melting away.

Since this virtual paradise is with you wherever you go, you can visit for a short time whenever you need a mini-vacation. Even two or three minutes can clear your mind. If you wish you can return to the exact same place, or you can decide that you prefer variety and each time you visit you will create new details.

If you ever find yourself in a place that is especially challenging to your level of serenity, mentally visit your personal utopia. The serenity you take back with you will make you glad you made the trip.

29

Emunah and Bitachon: The Foundation of Serenity

*A*wareness that the Almighty loves you, cares about your welfare, and orchestrates events in your life for your ultimate benefit is a powerful foundation upon which to build your life. Integrating *emunah* (awareness of the Almighty) and *bitachon* (trust in Him) results in a life of joy and serenity.

What will be in the future? Of course, you do not know the details. But *emunah* and *bitachon* give you the realization that what happens is meaningful and purposeful. You calmly face the challenges of the present and the future with an inner peace of mind. Those who demand that events must turn out exactly as they wish will feel nervous. What if things fail to work out that way? But those who wisely take action and at the same time leave the outcome to the infinite wisdom of their loving Father do have peace of mind.

How can you tell when you need to upgrade your level of *emunah* and *bitachon*? Your nervous system provides feedback. View anxiety and nervousness as a message, "Time to elevate your level of *emunah* and *bitachon*." Do not be upset by this. That surely is not very helpful. Rather, be appreciative of the feedback. The message you receive is immensely valuable.

"I have a great teacher for humility," the esteemed Rabbi told his students. "It's my nervous system. Whenever it registers anxiety because of worrisome thoughts, it teaches me that I have not yet reached the spiritual level that I strive for. While I would prefer to be on a higher level, I am grateful for a lesson in reality."

30

Connecting With the Creator

*T*he great scholar and sage, Rabbi Avraham Yeshaya Karelitz (*Chazon Ish* 1878-1953), wrote: "When a person merits becoming aware of the reality of the Almighty's existence, he will experience limitless joy. All of the pleasures of the flesh immediately disappear. His soul is enveloped in sanctity and it is as if he has left the body and floats in the upper Heavens. When a person transcends to this level, an entire new world is open to him. It is possible for a person to be momentarily like a celestial being in this world. All of the pleasures of this world are as nothing compared to the intense pleasure of a person cleaving to his Creator." (*Emunah U'bitachon*)

We have cited this frequently. It is such a powerful statement that it would be worthwhile reading it each and every day. Internalizing this awareness will lead to a life of serenity.

When you connect with the Creator, you will expand your consciousness of infinity and eternity. You will plug into the source of all serenity. Each time you recite a blessing, or pray, or perform a good deed, you will be connecting with your love for your Father, your King, Creator and Sustainer of the universe. You will be able to connect with the love that your Creator has for you. Gaining this awareness will add a spiritual dimension to all aspects of a person's life. Those who have integrated this live an elevated life and make wiser choices.

Do not expect to obtain this awareness easily and lightly. Be patient and approach this lofty goal serenely. As you reflect on this, little by little there will be progress. Do not be thrown off track by challenges. Do not expect a path of straight success. Setbacks are part of the journey. Persistence is the only way to reach any meaningful goal.

I felt discouraged. I had read about the importance of connecting with the Creator. This idea seemed absolutely great. But I was far from this. Every once in a while, I felt that I was connecting, but more often than not, I felt far away.

"The very fact that you are trying is what is expected," I was told. The verse tells us, 'Let there be joy in the heart of those who seek the Almighty' (Psalms 105:3). Allow yourself to experience joy for your very quest. Creating anxiety for yourself over this makes it even more difficult to get in touch with elevated thoughts and feelings. As you strive serenely, you will see that every step in the right direction will be a source of inspiration for further positive steps. Pray for the spiritual awareness that you desire. Appreciate the connectedness that you accomplish with these prayers."

31

Prayer: Daily Exercises in Serenity

*D*aily prayer is an ongoing exercise in serenity. When we pray, we have a greater awareness that we are addressing our Father, our King, Creator and Sustainer of the universe. We connect with the consciousness that *ein ode milvado*; that is, nothing else exists besides Him. Our very lives and welfare are totally a gift from the Almighty.

One of the issues of daily prayer is how to keep one's attention on the words one is saying. Minds easily wander. Some more easily than others. Problems and worries may divert one's attention. All forms of emotional issues may arise. This is exactly why prayer is an exercise in serenity. You need to free your mind from all bothersome thoughts and focus on the words of prayer. It is almost impossible for most people's minds to remain focused. The goal is to consistently bring back the focus to the prayers one is saying.

When you pray properly, you build up your ability to filter out everything in the environment. This is exactly what you need to do to attain serenity. In a serene state your mind resonates with the spiritual. The words of prayer take on a deeper meaning. As you are communicating with the Creator, you are elevating yourself. This will make it easier to maintain serenity. You realize that you are part of the Creator's world and you increase your trust in Him. This trust frees you from many of the factors that get in the way of serenity. Experiencing it on a heartfelt level gives you peace of mind. You know that you are in the hands of your loving Father and powerful King and you feel at ease.

A serene elderly person once told me, "When I was a young man I was the nervous type. To say that I lacked serenity would have been a gross understatement. I went to speak to a righteous scholar for advice.

"'You pray, don't you?' he asked me.

"'Of course,' I replied. 'But what should I do to make myself calmer?'

"'Pray,' he smiled.

"'But that hasn't helped me with my worrying and general nervousness,' I complained.

"'I bless you that your prayers should be a source of inner peace,' he said.

"This blessing immediately made me calmer. Carrying this blessing with me transformed my prayers into a high-

ly effective source of serenity. When I went back to thank him for his blessing, he said, 'It's not my blessing that helped you. It's the Almighty's blessing. He wants us to pray to Him for many benefits. Becoming more serene is one of them.'"

32

Shabbos:
The Day of Serenity

*T*he Torah tells us to celebrate the Creation of the universe one day each week. In the beginning of Creation, the world was lacking *"menuchah"* — a total day of rest. Shabbos, the seventh day of the week, was created to complete the Creation. Each week we once again commemorate the most amazing event in history. By resting on this day, we make a statement acknowledging the Creator's creation.

Even for Sabbath observers it is a challenge to keep to the spirit of Shabbos. This requires an inner serenity. One is required to view all of one's weekday work as if it has been completely finished. This is a mental exercise that will enable those who master it to be more serene the entire week.

When someone takes an actual trip to a scenic spot conducive for serenity, whenever he mentions or hears the name of that place his mind will replay those mental pictures either consciously or unconsciously and this helps access serene feelings. If one were using a biofeedback machine, one would clearly observe the stress level go down. Biofeedback machines measure muscle tension when one experiences stress. Your muscles give off more electricity, measured in microvolts, when they are tight, and less electricity when they are relaxed. Seeing this in front of you can be highly motivating to increase serene mental pictures.

When one observes Shabbos with a total sense of serenity, every time one thinks of Shabbos, one will feel more peaceful.

Some Shabbos observers focus on all the preparations they need to do for Shabbos and feel tense about this. Mentally go beyond the work involved. Remember that on Shabbos you will celebrate all that you have, all that exists on our planet, and all that exists in the entire cosmos. This is mind boggling. Let the joy and serenity of Shabbos permeate your being during your entire stay in this world.

Someone who wasn't personally familiar with the Torah way of observing Shabbos wrote that he had always viewed it as a day of restriction and limitation. It was a day when one is expected to refrain from many activities. He had once visited an institution in a city far from his home where he practiced a standard meditation. He found the exercises calming and relaxing. He felt a deeper sense of relaxation than he ever had previously. Prior to returning to his home city, he had the opportunity to observe a traditional Shabbos at the home of a Rabbi. He wrote that whatever that he had gained from meditation was only a miniature Jewish Shabbos. He acknowledged that his previous negative perception had been entirely wrong. He realized that Shabbos, when observed with the proper attitude, is a dynamic experience of serenity.

33

You Are a Soul

O nly bodies experience stress. Souls are serene. Identify with your soul; stress and tension will melt away.

Your essence is not your negative thoughts and distressful feelings. Your essence is your soul. If you are stressed, or tense, or worried, or frustrated, or upset, mentally step back and observe your thoughts and feelings. This will immediately help you gain a more objective perspective.

What does your soul really want? What choices and decisions would your soul make? Even if you do not yet have an exact answer, just thinking about this enables you to become more serene. When you quiet your mind and calm your body, i.e. your muscles, your soul's wisdom is more accessible.

When you perceive the entire picture from your soul's perspective many things that seem important to your physical self change their priority. Your body may be upset over a triviality or minor distress. To your soul this matter may be even less than trivial or minor. Seeing things from your soul's perspective, you will connect with the Creator. You will experience love for Him and gratitude for all that He gave you. A loving and grateful heart is a serene heart.

My husband and I cared about each other deeply. But we frequently caused each other much distress. We were experts at putting one another in negative states. It was suggested to us to say things that would elicit positive states. We tried half-heartedly and often felt discouraged.

Then we were told, "You aren't your negative thoughts and feelings. You are a soul. Treat each other in ways consistent with your soul's wisdom."

This reversed our lives in ways that we wouldn't have believed possible.

34

"Let There Be Light"

There was total darkness in the world until the Creator said, "Let there be light." The Torah states this at the very beginning, said the Chofetz Chaim, to tell us that even in the darkest periods of life, in a flash the Almighty can create light. Repeating these words will bring much light into your life.

Let the image of serene light be a source of creating positive energy for you. Visualize white light traveling from your head to your toes. Feel all your muscles relaxing. Feel every cell in your body vibrating with healthy energy. Feel that healthy energy recycling again and again. Let this empower you.

Breathe slowly and deeply as you reflect on the words, "Let there be light." As an exercise, see the effects of doing this for at least twenty minutes. If your mind wanders, calmly bring it back as you continue to slowly inhale and exhale. This can be a valuable tool for those who experience high levels of stress and anxiety. Feel these feelings melting away, as you imagine and experience the serenity of a soothing light. Words cannot adequately describe the actual experience of the calm and relaxed state you will have achieved after doing this for at least twenty minutes. So before you pass judgment whether this is for you, try it. A warning: If you repeat to yourself that this will not work for you, you will not be following instructions. The main benefit derives from clearing your mind of all thoughts other than, "Let there be light."

When turning on a light switch, repeat, "Let there be light." This will connect you with the original light of Creation. Connecting with the Creator will enable you to experience a greater inner peace and clarity of thought. This gives a broader, comprehensive context to your entire life.

A young gentleman who was new to his Jewish heritage told me, "I used to meditate a lot and found this a source of serenity. I haven't practiced this recently and I miss it. What can I do?"

I told him about the possibility of closing his eyes and repeating slowly, "Let there be light." Along with the awareness described by the Chofetz Chaim, this will help him to integrate a valuable message. One month later he reported that he did this twenty minutes a day and it was even more beneficial for him than what he had previously done.

35

The Spiritual "Tikun"

There is a spiritual concept of *"tikun"* that gives us a perspective conducive for serenity. Kabbalistically the term *"tikun"* means "rectification." Difficult and distressful life situations serve as a rectification for one's soul. A person accepts, and is even grateful for, medical treatment that heals and cures even though it can be painful. So, too, knowing that the challenges one faces serve as a benefit for one's eternal soul makes it easier to maintain serenity when facing difficulties.

Those who react to adversity and difficult situations with an attitude of, "Why me?" or, "This is a totally negative occurrence," experience increased stress and emotional suffering. Knowing that the adversity or difficulty is accomplishing something of major significance for you gives you the courage and inner strength to cope with what otherwise might be overwhelming. It still might not be easy, but it is much easier than it would have been without this realization.

Even if we do not know the precise dynamics of this *"tikun,"* being aware that there is a profound spiritual gain adds a spiritual dimension to our life. We do not deny the extent of the difficulty, but we do feel that we grow from it. And since it is our perception that is the key factor in the severity of our suffering, the *"tikun"* consciousness makes our burden lighter.

"I was suffering more than I ever imagined that I would," the middle-aged gentlemen said after he was asked about his life. "I had health concerns. I rarely felt well, even though I wasn't suffering from a life-threatening sickness. My financial situation was never to my liking, and I worried about how I would manage when my earning ability would decrease. I had family problems and in general I tended to be a bit depressed. It was suggested to me to speak to a distinguished, elderly Rabbi. I pushed off going to speak to him. Other things I had heard before did not help me for very long. I would become inspired every now and then, but the inspiration would dissipate and the suffering would return.*

"A friend of mine kept insisting that I go and eventually I felt that it was easier for me to get the meeting over and done with rather than having to listen to my friend's repetitious sales pitch.

"I would summarize the essence of what I was told as, 'Your difficulties are all part of the Almighty's plan for your tikun in this world. Accept it with joy.' This was a bit different than the approaches I was used to. At first I could

not tell how it was helpful. But I saw that whenever I was about to complain to others or even to myself, I reheard this righteous man's statement. I was not aware of the extent of the positive effects until several people who knew me well commented on how much calmer I was than ever before. I share my story with others since I know how much this helped me."

36

Guard Your Health

*T*here is a Torah commandment to guard our health. Elevated levels of stress cause many health problems. Your immune system operates optimally when you are calm and serene. The efforts one makes to alleviate stress is the fulfillment of the Creator's will. As our loving Father, He wants us to be well.

Viewing decreasing stress and increasing serenity as a spiritual obligation will prioritize it. Moreover, we should strive to experience joy in doing the Almighty's will (in Hebrew this is called *Simchah shel mitzvah*). This adds a major dimension to the entire process.

What if you do not spontaneously feel this joy? There is the often-quoted statement of Rabbi Moshe Chaim Luzzatto in *Mesilas Yesharim* (*Path of the Just*), Chapter Seven. The way you act externally has an effect on your inner emotions. Acting joyously will arouse positive inner feelings. Even if at first you do not spontaneously feel joyous about what you will be doing to master serenity, act as if you were joyful and allow those feelings to eventually become integrated and spontaneous.

There was a righteous man in Jerusalem who waited for red lights when crossing the street with the same fervor as when praying. Someone noticed the spiritual look on his face when he waited for the light to change and asked him about it.

"Whenever I wait for the light to change, I am fulfilling the Torah commandment to guard my health. This is a mitzvah (good deed) like any other."

Someone who heard this began to experience a similar spiritual awareness whenever he breathed slowly and deeply to alleviate stress and become more serene. He, too, was fulfilling the commandment to guard his health.

37

Calming Your Mind With "Serenity"

"Calm your mind." Practicing this skill is a major stepping stone to mastery of serenity. We all have a constant stream of thoughts that surface automatically. Some of these may be beneficial. For many, however, their stream of consciousness is the source of distress and unresourceful emotional states. Calming your mind enables you to experience serenity.

An easy-to-apply tool to help you calm your mind is to soothingly repeat the word "serenity" over and over again. By focusing your attention on this calming word, your mind is free from thoughts that are not conducive to serenity.

It is advisable to practice repeating "serenity" in a serene environment. Go to a garden or a room with soothing pictures and breathe slowly. Repeat the word "serenity" over and over again. Scan all your muscles and release all tension. By doing this, you create an association in your brain between repeating the word "serenity" and actually experiencing it.

A friend recently told me that a physician told him that it's imperative for him to reduce his level of stress. His blood pressure was too high, and his family had a history of heart problems.

I suggested that he practice repeating "serenity" twenty minutes a day while breathing slowly and deeply.

"But I'll climb the walls with frustration if I do that," he said. "It sounds excruciatingly boring."

"Have you ever tried this?" I asked.

"Of course not," he replied.

I insisted that for his health he had to at least try it out. He did, and then remarked, "I never would have imagined that I would be doing something like this. I had no idea that it would relax my entire being the way it does. I thought that it would be painfully boring. But when I actually practiced this, it was easier and more enjoyable that I had thought."

38

Create a Mental Shield

*E*ven after you are a master at creating serene states for yourself, there will always be external challenges. The negative words of others and the negative energy of others can have an effect on your state.

Protect yourself. Create a mental shield that will keep out negative energy and will enable you to remain in a state of a clear mind with relaxed muscles.

Imagine yourself surrounded by a protective shield. You might want this to be like a thick plastic bubble. This will let in positive words and energy but keep out negative influences. You may prefer to imagine being surrounded by light that increases your serenity at the same time it prevents anything negative from affecting you.

You may want to imagine a special cloak that protects you. Since it is your imagination, you can create any variation that you find beneficial.

Ultimately it is your mind that you are programming to keep out the negative energy. By imagining a protective shield you have a helpful tool that makes it easier for your mind to keep out negativity.

I spoke to someone who was an expert at maintaining serenity. I knew that he often was in challenging environments and I asked him how he does it.

"With my imagination I have created a special transformer. This transforms any negative words or energy that come my way and turns them into positive words of encouragement and serene empowerment. Any negative energy is transformed into positive energy."

If you are dealing with challenging situations, mentally create your own transformer. It is free and you do not have to know anything about technology or engineering to create it with your imagination.

39

Techniques for Serenity

*I*nternalizing the attitudes that create serenity builds a sturdy foundation for serenity. Together with this, having techniques available adds to your ability to maintain serenity even during challenging moments. Here we will list some. Try them out for yourself. Having one technique that works for you can be better than just reading an entire catalogue of tools. Experiment with techniques. You may creatively make some variations and then the technique will work for you in ways that are more effective.

- "Now I am aware ..." technique. Start sentence after sentence with the words "Now I am aware ..." Look around you and mention various objects or sights that you are aware of. This takes your brain away from focusing on the past or future or on thoughts that are stressful and you focus on neutral things that you are presently aware of.

- Mentally travel up and down your muscle infrastructure and let each and every muscle relax. You can say to each muscle, "Relax." Say this in a calm, soothing voice.

- When you are tense or nervous, stop thinking all thoughts for a few minutes and just be aware of the tension in your muscles from head to toe. Nonjudgmentally just be aware of your consciousness being inside those muscles. This itself causes your muscles to relax.
- Circle of serenity technique. Imagine a large circle in front of you or at the side. Inside this circle visualize masters of serenity one by one leaving their serenity inside. Feel a tremendous amount of serenity stored up. Mentally step into this circle and feel that serenity permeating your being from head to toe. Whenever you need some more serenity step inside again.
- Imagine a special laser machine with beams of serenity-creating light. See yourself sitting or standing in front of this machine. See the rays of light bombarding your brain with serenity. You can close your eyes and feel the soothing serenity.
- Mental pool of serenity. Imagine a pool filled with serenity-creating water. Whenever you need to immerse yourself with serenity take a virtual swim in this pool. Feel all stress and tension melting away every time you enter this pool.
- Mental shower of serenity. Imagine stepping into a shower that in place of water has serene light giving you a shower of serenity. Instead of ending up wet, you end up serene.
- Mentally don the head of a master of serenity. Visualize that person and then imagine placing that person's head over

yours. This makes it easier for you to model that person by thinking the thoughts you project that person would be thinking. That person's serenity becomes your serenity also.

- Put your hands on a tree. Feel all stress and tension leaving you and traveling down the tree, through its roots, and into the ground. Feel calm and relaxing feelings coming up from the ground leaving you calm and refreshed.
- Imagine yourself as a swan floating serenely on a peaceful lake on a perfectly pleasant day.
- Imagine being a bird flying serenely from one beautiful garden to another.
- Imagine being near a waterfall. Watch the water cascading and feel yourself becoming totally serene.
- Keep a scrapbook of peaceful scenes that you can look at. Close your eyes and feel the way you would feel if you were actually there.
- Stretch out your arms and move them around in all different directions. Then feel positive energy from the entire universe flowing through your arms to every part of your nervous system. Feel the great energy vibrating throughout your entire system. You can move your hands round and round causing this energy to become stronger and stronger.

40

Music Changes States

*I*t was late at night. We were traveling a long distance on an interstate highway and suddenly a major storm broke out. The torrential rains blocked visibility. The driver was taken aback since the weather had been pleasant all day and had changed drastically seemingly without warning.

"This is terrible," said the driver. Trucks and cars speeded by while he found it more and more difficult to stay in his lane. He became more anxious with each passing mile. He couldn't see well at night and missed the exit he needed.

"This is a nightmare," he said with panic in his voice. "We are on the wrong road, and driving conditions are terrible. I don't know where we are."

I realized I had to help him change his state to a much calmer one and I had to do it quickly and smoothly.

"What songs do you enjoy?" I asked.

He took a tape of some of his favorite music and started to play it. He immediately calmed down. He stopped making counterproductive statements about how awful the *weather and driving conditions were, and felt much more relaxed. He sang along with the tape and his entire state was totally changed. He now said calmly, "I'll enjoy the music while I drive carefully. Eventually we'll get to where we need to go."*

We arrived safely and he saw how quickly he could change his state from high levels of stress to being calm and relaxed even though the external conditions were challenging.

Music is enjoyable because of its power to put us in positive states. Every time a specific song or tune puts you in an especially positive and resourceful state, make a mental note of it. When you are experiencing stress, sing that song, hum that tune, or play it on a tape recorder. Even when this is not possible, many people find that in their mind they can hear the song or music.

Because music is such a powerful tool for change, it is important to avoid music that has negative effects and to utilize soothing and elevating music that is conducive for serenity.

41

How Did You Do It?

*T*here is a helpful technique that is known as the "How did you do it?" technique. The way to apply this to achieve serenity is to imagine that you are already serene. Then ask yourself, "How did I manage to do it?"

You can apply this tool to specific instances when you want to become serene. And you can apply this to an expert mastery of serenity. Use your ability to imagine. Now imagine yourself being serene. From the vantage point of already being serene look back and see what you said, thought, and did that enabled you to be serene.

This technique has an effect similar to the NLP question: "If you did know, what would the answer be?" In the context of serenity, suppose someone claims, "I don't know what to do to make myself serene right now." Then you can ask, "If you did know, what do you think you could do?"

This question is helpful because almost everyone knows more about certain things than they realize. Asking the question helps them overcome blocking their magnificent memory bank and their creativity. Similarly, by imagining that you are already serene you remember and create more than you otherwise would have.

The question asked in this chapter can also be used for instances when we are presently stuck but we are aware that in certain contexts we have been serene. Ask yourself about the contexts where you have been serene, "How did I do it?" You know without a doubt that you already did it. How? Your answer will enable you to be serene right now.

Develop the habit of asking people who are skilled at doing things, "How did you do it?" By listening to the answers of many people, you will be able to increase the amount of times you will be able to answer this for others.

42

Serenity Coach

*I*n every important area of life we do better when we have a coach. A coach has a more objective view and will be able to point out ways that we can improve.

Very often, the people who need coaches the most refuse to consult anyone. They may feel that asking someone for help is a sign of weakness. They may feel an inner need to consider themselves complete and perfect. Experts usually understand that they have a lot to gain from knowledgeable people. Even if other people do not have more knowledge, since they are more objective, their input could be valuable.

A serenity coach could be someone who is a model of serenity. Or it could be anyone who observes us and points out to us when we need to return to a more serene state. Others view our facial reactions, which we cannot see unless we are looking into a mirror, and therefore observe the biofeedback that is expressed on our faces. If you have an opportunity to benefit from someone who agrees to be your coach, it makes sense that you should not pass up the opportunity.

You can even create your own mental-serenity coach. Visualize someone who will serve as coach. It could be someone you know, or have heard of, or have created in your imagination. Ultimately this is a way that you access your inner wisdom. Deep down you know when you need to change your thoughts or your states. Your virtual coach will remind you to do so.

I asked a person who personified serenity how he became so serene.

"I owe it all to my serenity teacher," he said.

"And how did he develop his serenity?" I asked.

"He wasn't serene at all," the person said with a smile. "His personality got on my nerves to a great degree. I figured that if I could be serene in his presence I could always be serene. So I was totally committed to maintain a serene state whenever I was in his presence. And once I mastered this, I knew that all the more so I could be serene in the presence of anyone else."

"I didn't feel it was practical to have an actual coach to help me alleviate stress, so I bought a biofeedback machine," the once stressed-out physician told me. "I had trouble with my heart and realized that I had to do whatever it takes to learn to decrease my stress level. Every evening I would practice for at least twenty minutes, mentally visualizing relaxing scenes. 'It's time for my session with my coach,' I

would jokingly say. The biofeedback machine immediately measured the rise and fall of my stress level. Every thought and mental picture either increased or decreased my level of stress. Having a clear picture of what was happening enabled me to gain the skill to control my thoughts and mental pictures even when I was not hooked up to the biofeedback machine."

43

Letting Off Steam

At times you may be so upset, frustrated, and stressed that you must let off steam before you will feel ready to try to access serenity. You want to let go of your distressful feelings or at least to make them lighter.

The easiest tool you always have at your disposal is breathing slowly and deeply. As you breathe, feel the tension and stress leaving. You may do this by counting down from 20 to 1 and after each number repeat to yourself, "Deeper and deeper relaxed. Deeper and deeper relaxed." When you are extremely stressed out, you may want to count from 100 to zero. Or you may want to breath slowly and deeply without counting. Try these and see which is preferable for you.

Another tool for letting off steam is to write down your thoughts and feelings on a piece of paper or type it on a computer. As you express yourself in writing, you will be lightening your burden.

Another tool is to use the two-chair method. Speak to an imaginary person in another chair. After you have expressed yourself, switch chairs and respond to what was said when you were in your original chair as if you were someone else speaking to you. For many, this has proven to be a highly effective tool.

Some people find it helpful to speak to themselves in a mirror. Describe how you are feeling. After a while you can begin to describe how you would prefer to feel. Then you can act the way you would be acting if you were joyous, even vibrantly and enthusiastically ecstatic. As you see yourself being this way in a mirror you have a powerful biofeedback machine.

Physical exercise is a healthy way to let off steam. You might try walking briskly, running, jumping, or swimming. Even if it will be a while until you are actually able to engage in physical exercise, having had experiences when this has already been helpful for you will help you calm down a bit because you know that in "x" amount of time you will alleviate your stress or anxiety with exercise.

Speaking to an understanding friend can help you let off steam. We intentionally listed the other tools first, since those are approaches that you can do on your own. When you speak to someone else, be aware of your goal. Your desired outcome is to decrease your level of stress. It is beneficial to state this right at the beginning. This will escalate the process and could prevent the conversation from making you even more stressed than before you began speaking.

44

Melting the Stress of Past Memories

*W*henever we remember an event or incident from the past, we once again experience some of the feelings associated with those memories. When we remember joyous moments, we feel happy (unless we look at them with a negative frame in the present). When we remember distressful moments of the past, we feel part of that distress in the present.

The good news is that when you are able to put yourself into a serene state and are able to maintain it, you can now melt the stress of those memories. This process is known as desensitization. By staying in a totally serene state, those past memories now become associated with feelings of inner calm.

Some people find this easier to do if they mentally dissociate themselves from distressful memories. They therefore view the memories as if those mental pictures were on a screen or as if they were a play on a stage. Some people use a double dissociation. That is, they imagine they are up in a balcony and are watching themselves in the audience watching themselves on a screen. The principle is: By reviewing the memories when you are serene, they lose their power to continue to cause distress.

If while trying this method you feel anxiety, just relax. You are presently safe. Keep breathing slowly and deeply and repeat the word, "serenity." If necessary, mentally travel to a serene haven, a garden, or any similar place. Add the positive states of courage and serene empowerment. Feel joy that you are gaining greater mastery over your brain.

When you first try, do this with memories that are only minimally distressful. As you build up your confidence in your ability to do this effectively, you will be able to apply this to any memory, even those that used to have highly stressful effects.

For individuals with highly intense reactions, it is worthwhile to consult a competent professional who is knowledgeable in these patterns.

45

Bothersome Thoughts

*D*o not expect to have perfect mastery over your thoughts. This is not realistic. Every person will have unwanted thoughts. These are thoughts that create anxiety and stress. Besides the stress these thoughts create in themselves, you might feel bad that you do not have the mastery over your thoughts that you desire.

The skill to master is to move on to the type of thoughts that you want for yourself. Do not fight the thoughts you do not want. That keeps them at the forefront of your consciousness. Gently and lightly move on to focus on something else.

We have previously discussed the power of using the word, "Next." Say, "Next!" and then think of something else. Practice this now. Think of something, then say, "Next!" and think of something else. Try this at least ten times and see how it works. By practicing many times, you will find this tool highly effective.

Be prepared with thoughts, ideas, and imagery on which you can focus. It is helpful to write a list for yourself and then review that list when you need it. In my book, *"Patience,"* I wrote that keeping a written list of times and moments when you were in resourceful states is beneficial. Give each of those states a unique title. For example, you might have a state, "Joyous wedding state," "Serene botanical gardens state," "Exhilarating view from top of mountain state." Reading this list, to which you can keep adding, will be a great way to focus on memories and thoughts that are conducive for resourceful states.

There are individuals who are highly idealistic and want to think elevated thoughts consistently. This is so important to them that they become obsessed with negative thoughts. Their obsessive thoughts become so strong that the more they try not to think of them the more those thoughts get stuck in their minds like a broken record. Rabbi Yaakov Greenwald, a religious psychologist, has written a book in Hebrew (Eitzos VeHadrachos) dealing with religious obsessions. He cites personal letters he received on the subject from the Steipler Gaon Rabbi Yaakov Yisrael Kanievsky, author of the Talmudic works, Kehillas Yaakov. This topic and the approach is so important that he received letters of approbation from major Torah authorities.

To summarize the basic concept: A person is not to blame for unwanted thoughts that he tries to overcome but that nevertheless keep coming back. Obsessive thoughts are really a medical and psychological issue and not a religious one. By taking a calm approach, you will be more relaxed and even though it will take time to overcome the problem, eventually you will. When obsessive thoughts are over-whelming, a professional who is an expert in this field should be consulted.

46

Serenity Is Contagious

*B*eing in the presence of someone who is serene makes one more serene. Emotional energy is contagious. Someone who is angry and bitter causes distress for those close by. Being near someone who is joyous makes one feel happier. For this reason people who are joyously serene are a pleasure to be with. Their positive energy effects your own energy positively.

We can derive two principles from this. First, be near serene people as often as you can. If you are feeling especially frazzled, think of someone you can speak to in person or on the telephone who is serene. Even a brief encounter with a cheerfully serene salesperson or clerk will have a beneficial effect.

Secondly, you owe it to others to decrease your level of stress and upgrade your level of serenity. Serene teachers have a serene effect on their students. Serene parents have a serene effect on their children. Serene employers have a serene effect on employees. By being cheerfully serene you will have a beneficial effect on everyone you pass and greet in the workplace.

Be aware of people whose negative energy effects you negatively. Be resolved to be such a powerful force for the good that your positive energy will influence them instead of them influencing you.

Someone told me that he used to be very confused about his emotional states. Throughout the day he experienced a roller coaster of ups and downs. He was not aware of any special problems. The thoughts he was aware of could not account for such erratic fluctuations.

He spoke to a number of people who had different theories, some making more sense than others. But it took a while for him to figure out the cause.

He eventually realized that he was highly sensitive to the emotional states of others, much more than the norm. When he was around calm, happy people he immediately felt calmer and happier. When in the presence of people who were in unresourceful states, he immediately felt diminished or nervous energy. Just realizing this made him feel much better. Afterwards, when in the presence of negative energy, he consciously bombarded his mind with thoughts and memories that would empower him. This made him much less vulnerable.

47

Harmonious Communication

$\mathcal{S}$ome people are experts at provoking others. The way they communicate gets others irritated, frustrated, and angry. Even when they basically agree, they sound as if they are arguing.

Experts at harmonious communication begin their conversation with words of agreement. They open their own statements by commenting on the points which with they agree. Even if what they agree on is of minor significance, they will first say something to the effect of, "I see that we agree that ..." This builds rapport.

Most people are able to communicate harmoniously with some individuals and find this challenging with others. Learn from your own moments of strength and success. How do you speak and what do you say when you experience harmony? Think of the people with whom you lack harmony. Mentally see yourself speaking harmoniously with those people. In what ways does this differ from the way you actually speak to them? Be resolved to avoid patterns that create friction and to speak in ways that create harmony.

Many people needlessly say things that just get the person they are talking to upset or irritated without there being any actual benefit. As we have stated in previous books, before speaking focus on the outcome you want. Be totally resolved not to say needless words that just cause distress and are counterproductive. Choosing your words carefully can take a lot of effort. Making that effort is elevating.

If you find a specific individual especially challenging, learn from those who are able to interact harmoniously with him. If necessary, consult an expert in communication.

A manager at a large company was on the verge of divorce. He and his wife bickered a lot. "I just don't know how to talk to her without quarreling," he often said.

"How do you speak to difficult employees?" he was asked. "Do you scream at them or threaten to fire them?"

"Of course not," he said. "I express appreciation for the work they have already done. I show them that I respect them. I keep my tone of voice pleasant and I only say what I think will be beneficial."

"If you would speak to your wife this way, do you think you would have more harmony?"

"That makes sense," he said.

He agreed to try to create harmony at home. Since he had already communicated this way many times at his company, once he was aware of what he needed to do at home and was determined to follow through, he found it easier than he would have previously imagined to greatly improve the way he spoke.

48

Frustrations Can Lead to Serenity

*T*he very nature of being on our planet is that minor and trivial frustrations occur frequently. Some people overreact greatly. Others get highly annoyed when frustrations pile up. And yet others are able to let them go. "It's really nothing," they say out loud or to themselves.

There is a well-known statement "Frustration leads to anger" that might be statistically true but is not a law of nature. As a matter of fact experiencing frustration is a mild form of anger. But what will frustration really lead to?

Frustration will lead to any quality with which you consistently associate it. That means, you as a thinking human being have the ability of creating a new chain of emotional states. If every time you felt frustrated, you would find something humorous in the situation, then you personally would have the pattern of "Frustration leads to laughter." If every time you felt frustrated, you would consciously make an effort to remember something you were grateful for, then you personally have the pattern of "Frustration leads to gratitude." And in the context of this book, you can create your own pattern of "Frustration leads to serenity."

How will you create gratitude from frustration? Every time something frustrating happens, ask yourself, "What am I grateful for?" You could say to yourself, "The only reason I'm frustrated is because I am alive, I am grateful to be alive." Or, you could find something else to be grateful for each time. You can be grateful for being able to see, hear, walk, talk, or think. When will it become automatic? Only you will be able to answer this for yourself, so build up your curiosity and experiment. You will be grateful you did.

How will you create serenity from frustration? Every time you feel frustrated, you will begin to tell yourself, "The only reason this frustrates me is because of the thoughts that I am thinking. I will let those thoughts go and I will come back to the present." This will give you many opportunities to soothe your mind. Enjoy the process. Do not try to do this perfectly. The more frustrating occurrences you experience in your life, the more practice you will have at being serene.

When I first heard about the idea of frustrations leading to serenity, I was skeptical. This hadn't been my experience in the past. But I was advised to try it out. It didn't work that well for me and I complained to the person who advised it.

"O.k., let's find a variation of this that might work better for you," I was told. "How about clapping your hands, snapping your fingers, and saying, 'Great, this is going to make me serene.'"

I laughed when I heard this. "Great," I was told, "this is working for you already." When I did this on a regular basis, I found it highly effective.

49

Physical Factors

*T*here are many physical factors that will have an influence on one's states in general, and on serenity in particular. Being well rested is conducive to serenity, being tired and worn out is not. Eating healthful foods and in the right amounts is conducive to serenity, eating improperly is not. Exercising moderately is conducive to serenity, lack of any exercise is not. Healthiness is conducive to serenity, illness is not.

Sufficient rest, proper eating habits, and adequate exercise are areas where we can try to take charge. Health and illness may often be beyond our control. Even so, serenity makes it easier to cope with illness and can be an important ingredient in a comprehensive health program.

Food allergies and other sensitivities can be the source of a lack of serenity. Many people are allergic to white sugar and white flour even though they do not realize it. Those who have high levels of anxiety should confer with experts to see if changing their diet could have a beneficial effect on their serenity level.

The entire subject of mind-body connection is at the present in early stages of development with many diverse opinions among knowledgeable professionals. Even where a physical factor is present that makes it more difficult to be serene, with greater mastery of one's thoughts and imagery one can transcend potential obstacles.

Drinking water is known to have a calming effect on the nervous system. This can be increased by mindfully reciting a blessing thanking the Almighty for the gift of water. Also, as you are drinking the water visualize a relaxing scene and say to yourself, "This, too, will make me more and more serene with each and every sip." If you want to calm yourself and you do not have water available, virtual water can also be helpful. Imagine drinking water taken directly from a natural mountain spring and feel the calm feelings as the imaginary water enters your system. Of course, with only virtual water one can become dehydrated so remember to also drink actual water. Some people imagine that this form of imagination is not for them so they mentally block it from working. When they realize that it is their brain's subjective thoughts that are preventing this, they will be more open to utilizing the power of their mental imagery.

50

Write It Down

When something is weighing heavily on your mind, write it down. When you find it difficult to make a decision, write it down. Whenever you find your mind going around and around in circles, write it down. When overwhelmed with what you have to do, write it down.

When you take what is going on in your brain and put it on paper (or a computer), you now can look at it more objectively. Your mind will feel lighter. You can more easily weigh the pros and cons of a potential decision. If those same pros and cons are a mishmash in your thoughts, they might jump back and forth like a Ping-Pong ball. Several factors on each side of an issue may be repeated so many times that they could seem like several hundred. After you write down the essence of each point in separate columns for the pros and cons, you will find it easier to evaluate the merits of all positions. You might even think of new alternatives. Even before you reach a practical decision, you will be clear about the relevant factors that need to be evaluated.

When you have so much to do that you feel as if you are carrying a heavy mountain on your shoulders, write down your "to do" list. You may have to take care of various items in different locations. If so, make a separate column for each location or type of activity (for example, home, office, school, buy, call). Then think objectively: What has a high priority to be done and what has a lower priority? Your "absolutely must do" list may be shorter.

Problems written on paper can become more solvable as you list possible solutions. By brainstorming and writing down even potential solutions that seem unlikely to be practical, you still will begin to get the feeling that the problem could have a solution. Even before an actual solution comes up, you will feel calmer that you are going in the right direction.

"I don't have enough time to write things down," I told my friend who suggested this to me. "I'm so busy I can't be bothered by writing anything."

"I used to think the same thing," he admitted. "But I found that writing things down saves me a lot of time."

I realized that my friend accomplished more than I did, so I developed the habit of writing things down. Decisions were arrived at more easily, more things got done with fewer oversights, and I became a calmer person. I am an advocate for writing things down and consider convincing others of its value a major contribution to their lives.

51
Facing Challenges Serenely

"**E**verything in our lives is meant to be a challenge to help us grow." This is the perspective to life by the great scholar and kabbalist, Rabbi Moshe Chaim Luzzatto, in the first chapter of his classic work *Mesillas Yesharim (Path of the Just)*. Facing your unique life challenges serenely will give you the clarity of thought to handle them at your best.

He tells us that wealth is a challenge and so is poverty. Health is a challenge and so is illness. When life goes smoothly it is meant to be a challenge and so are times one experiences adversity.

It is as if a driver or pilot in training has a computerized simulator that indicates all sorts of difficulties. He needs to maintain a clear state of mind and relaxed muscles in order for his brain to function at its optimal level. If someone becomes nervous, worried, or overwhelmed, it is unlikely that he will do well. Many people marvel at the abilities of professional pilots and speed-car drivers to stay calm in life-threatening situations. But it is precisely this calm that makes it more likely that they will succeed.

How do you remain serene during a time of challenge? With mental practice. People who worry in advance about potential challenges are practicing. They are practicing becoming anxious and nervous. What you want for yourself is to practice maintaining serenity. Practice serenely. Every time you are faced with any challenge, repeat to yourself, "This is a challenge from which I will grow." You will develop your character with each and every challenge. Success is a challenge to your character and lack of success is a challenge. When things are going well it is a challenge, and when things are not at all the way you wish them to be it is a challenge.

Think back at any challenges in the past that you did not handle the way you would have wished. Now relive those challenges and see yourself serenely growing from those challenges. Any challenges you experienced in the past are still challenges in the present. View them with serenity and see yourself growing.

I met a person who had lost a fortune. Before the Second World War he was wealthy. He lost all the money he had and he lost his health. But he was consistently cheerful and calm. I wondered how he was able to be this way. Perhaps inside he was more ruffled than he looked.

"How is everything?" I heard someone ask him.

"I thank the Almighty for each and every day," he replied with a big smile.

"How's your business going?" was the next question.

"It's going exactly the way I need it to go," he said.

Looking back I realize that this was his secret. He knew that whatever the reality he faced, that reality was the challenge he needed for his continued spiritual growth.

52

Serenely Acknowledging Mistakes

$\mathcal{I}$t is impossible for a mortal to never make a mistake. This can give us a sense of humility. The more objective we are, the less we will defend our mistakes. A key reason why it is so difficult to acknowledge mistakes is because we feel an excessive amount of distress about the possibility of having been wrong.

A truth seeker makes it a higher priority to be correct, right, and accurate in the first place than to defend a mistake as not being a mistake. Those who place a high value on truth and accuracy find it easier to acknowledge mistakes serenely. Rather than dealing with high levels of stress at the thought of having to admit they were wrong, they feel positive about being on the right track now.

Many people are afraid to acknowledge mistakes because they think that this will cause others to look down at them. The reality is usually the opposite. Most people respect and admire those who have the elevated character trait of being able to remain serene when saying they were wrong.

It is worthwhile to practice repeating: "I see that I was wrong," and, "I made a mistake." By repeating them serenely right now, when you actually need them, you will be prepared.

I asked someone who was able to admit that he was wrong with a positive emotional state, "I have seen you acknowledge that your position is wrong with the same good spirit as when you feel that you are right. How are you able to do this?"

"I thank my parents for this," he said. "When I was growing up, they praised me and my siblings for admitting mistakes. I remember being told, 'It takes a greater person to say that he was wrong than to persistently argue that what one has said or done wasn't wrong.' Having grown up with this attitude, it's relatively easy for me to do this."

53

"Something Might Go Wrong"

"*How* ow can I ever be serene? Something might go wrong."
"*I have to be nervous. Things might not work out the way I was hoping they would.*"

"*I can't be certain that everything will go right. Unless I can be sure that it will, anxiety is inevitable.*"

It is certainly true that something may go wrong. But where is there a law of the universe that one cannot be serene in the present just because something may subsequently go wrong? And there is not even a universal law forbidding humans to be calm and serene when something does go wrong.

We need to plan ahead to try to prevent things from going wrong. We would be wise to plan ahead to figure out options of what we can do to improve things in case something does go wrong. And it is the intelligent thing to do to be in a calm state of alert mind, relaxed body (muscles), when something goes wrong. The ideal is to think as clearly and creatively as we can.

The ultimate solution to worrying about things going wrong is to master the ability to remain serene regardless of how things turn out. When you have mastered this, you never need to be nervous in advance worrying that something might not work out, because even if it actually does not work out you will still be serene.

"When even trivial things go wrong, I see that you become very upset. What stops you from taking matters calmly?" I asked a successful businessman.

"But if I'm too relaxed, even more things will go wrong," he replied earnestly. "If you don't stop a small leak in a ship, eventually the entire ship will sink."

"Your metaphor is certainly stating an accurate fact," I agreed. "But if a sailor is serene, he can still fix the 'leak,' can't he?"

"Of course. He probably will do better by being centered."

"Can you see how you will live a more peaceful life if you fix things calmly?" I asked. "You won't be nervous in advance. And you'll be more serene as you take corrective action."

"I guess it's because I grew up in a home where everyone got all bent out of shape when things went wrong. Objectively, it makes sense to deal with whatever happens calmly."

I hope it makes sense to you, too, dear reader.

54

Compassion and Serenity: A Balance

$\mathcal{S}$erenity enables you to be compassionate, and authentic compassion increases your serenity. Compassion is where you sincerely care about the welfare of others. You feel for the suffering of others and wish them to be healed and helped. If someone is going through a rough period of time, whether financially, emotionally, physically, or spiritually, you mentally join with them and their situation. Compassion leads to kind words and actions. When people who suffer are in the presence of someone with compassion, they feel better; their burden becomes a bit lighter. Compassion is an elevating attribute and with this quality you emulate the Creator.

An excessive amount of compassion can be overwhelming, so we need to develop a balance. Serenity enables you to be compassionate. When someone is emotionally stressed or upset, there isn't room to feel the suffering of others. "I have enough problems of my own, I can't hear about the difficulties of others," is what goes through many people's minds. A mind that is serene, however, is open. Feelings of compassion can cause distress, but this is a healthy feeling. One feels good about having these feelings.

Compassion increases serenity. When you resonate with care about other people, you are engaged in a spiritual experience. You connect with what is truly important in life. It is true that this can be unsettling; however, it results in growth and character development. Ultimately this enables one to be more serene. Pettiness and trivialities play less of a role in one's life. You are in touch with what is most important during your sojourn on this world. Compassion broadens your consciousness and gives you greater perspective.

When is one in a state of too much compassion? When one becomes excessively stressed. When one obsesses. When one cannot concentrate where concentration is necessary. A callous or apathetic person might consider even minimal doses of compassion as too much. The more serenely kind you are, the more compassion you will be able to handle. Increasing your capacity for serenity is a meaningful goal.

Someone in the later stages of a terminal illness told me, "Many people who have known me when I was well have shied away from me. I understand their feelings since I have to admit that I have been in similar situations in the past. I didn't know what to say. I didn't think that anything I could do or say would make a difference. Now that I have been ill for a while, I have a different perspective. I don't expect anyone to do the impossible. But every time I speak to someone who truly cares about me, it makes me feel much better. Even when total strangers have said kind words that come from the heart, it is precious to me. I don't want anyone to have pity on me. I don't want anyone to think that I am essentially different than them just because I am ill. The serene compassion of others enables me to be more serene myself. And this is what I need most right now."

55
Perfectionism and Serenity

*I*f you will wait until you are perfect to allow yourself to experience serenity, the chances are fairly good that you will never be serene. It makes sense to start by allowing yourself to be serene. This will not necessarily make you perfect. But you will do much better than if you were to experience needless tension and stress.

Serenity will enable you to focus on excellence and improvement. You will be able to feel the joy of progress. Progress itself can have its ups and downs. By regarding the search for excellence as a priority, you will have the resilience to continue to improve. The emotional state you will experience as you improve will be positive and resourceful.

If someone has an excessive need for perfection, the inner thoughts tend to be, "If I'm not totally perfect, I'm a failure." This either/or thinking creates havoc with one's emotions. In reality, there are numerous levels between being perfect and failing.

Look at a situation with objectivity to assess what and how you are presently doing. At times, you will find that the present level is satisfactory. Even if it is not, being coolly objective will enable you to evaluate what exactly you can do in the present to upgrade the quality of your work.

"If you don't do something well, don't do it at all." This was the motto I grew up with. Even though "well" was the word used, what was referred to was actually perfection. And since I found it impossible to do things 100 percent perfectly, I was invariably in a consistent state of tension. Even after I grew up and left home, this motto was strongly ingrained in my mind.

Someone noticed how tense I usually was and asked me about it.

"I'm a perfectionist," I said, as if that was an adequate explanation.

"I used to be one also," he said to me. "But I've learned from experience that by giving up on perfection, I'm able to do a lot better and I generally feel much calmer."

This is exactly what I needed to change my attitude. The person who told me this accomplished a tremendous amount. Much more than those who insisted that I do everything "well."

56

Plan? Yes.
Worry? No.

*T*he future is always unknown. Regardless of how much we plan, things might not work out the way we would have wished. And regardless of how much we worry, that is, feeling anxiety about the future, whatever will be will be and worrying will not change anything.

In order to master serenity, we need to think about the future serenely in the present. That means, worry is out. Worrying causes us to waste our present moments with distress about what might or might not be in the future. Since when you worry you are suffering now without improving anything, it makes sense that worrisome thoughts are not where you want to spend your time in this world.

The wise person visualizes the outcome (Talmud, *Tamid* 32a) and takes action to prevent problems and to improve situations. A serene mind is able to think more clearly about the wisest course of action.

Turn your mind away from worrisome thoughts. Focus on gratitude. Focus on joy. Focus on what you can do to accomplish your goals. Focus on your best moments and favorite states. Since your mind focuses only on one thing at a time, this will automatically free you from worry. When you can take constructive action, do so. Otherwise, benefit from and enjoy the present. Ultimately when the future becomes the present, you will make it more probable that you will cope with serenity. The future only exists when it becomes the present and you know how to be serene in the present.

"I ran a large business," the head of a major company related, "and if I wasn't going to worry, there were an uncountable number of things that could go wrong.

"My doctor warned me that my stress level was ruining my health. But I argued that I couldn't slow down. Too many people depended on me. The physician suggested that I speak to an elderly gentleman who was one of the calmest people one would ever meet.

"'I can't afford to waste my time and energy on worrying,' he told me. 'Too many people depend on me. My well-being effects the lives of others. I owe it to them to stay calm and plan with a clear head.'

"This changed my own attitude. I was dedicated to emulate this role model."

57

Blaming: An Enemy of Serenity

Be a blamer or be serene; you cannot be both. Blamers create negativity, resentment, and hostility. Besides the anguish they cause others, this pattern robs them of serenity. A blaming pattern of thinking is one that focuses on the negative. And the people they blame usually react with counterblaming, anger, and animosity. Just think about it: How do you personally react when you are faced with someone who has a strong blaming pattern?

When you want to get someone to take action or to upgrade the quality of their work, think of positive ways to motivate them. Those who blame others for what goes wrong might superficially seem to be trying to improve things, but ultimately their blaming will make things worse. The resentment this pattern causes will boomerang.

Children with blaming parents suffer. Students with blaming teachers suffer. Employees with blaming employers suffer.

Anyone who encounters a blaming person suffers. Never be the cause of suffering for others.

Learn to motivate, encourage, empower, and influence with positive words and with a positive tone of voice. Everyone has the need to point out mistakes and shortcomings at one time or another. Do it in a way that enables the recipient of your communication to feel good about the way you spoke to him.

When things are over and done with, blaming just creates distressful states. Nothing is gained and much can be lost. Develop the habit of not commenting unnecessarily.

Some people feel, "If I don't blame, others won't improve." This is mistaken thinking. There are many patterns from which to choose when you want to motivate and influence. Give feedback with suggestions on how to improve something without sounding accusatory or condemning. Speak in a voice that projects inner kindness and empathy. If you can only think of blaming in a negative way, you might be tempted to blame yourself for not learning more positive patterns of communication. But better yet, do not blame anyone, not even yourself. Rather, be highly motivated to win friends and influence people with patterns that are self-respecting and respectful of the other person. Have a vision of the heights people can attain. Then speak to them in ways that make them want to do what will bring them to excellence.

"I grew up in a blaming house," the chronic blamer explained. "That's all I know."

"Have you ever witnessed anyone ask another person to fix something in a positive manner?"

"Certainly," he replied.

"So the reality is that you have both positive role models and negative ones, isn't it?" he was challenged and he had to agree that he had observed both patterns.

"From now on, emulate those who are experts at influencing and motivating in ways that boost the self-image of others. You will accomplish much more in the long run." He followed this advice. You, the reader, would be wise to do the same.

"I was told to stop blaming," said the man who had been divorced four times. "But I can't let others say and do things that I don't like. If I don't tell them like it is, I won't be true to myself."

"What are you trying to accomplish by your blaming?" I asked him.

"I would like the people I blame to change. And even if they don't actually change, at least I am able to express my protest."

"What have you lost out by blaming?" I asked.

"That's a loaded question," he replied. "I can't help it if others are too weak to handle the truth."

"Picture yourself being serene and gently expressing yourself. When you've blamed others, your batting average of success hasn't been that great. I doubt if you will lose out by developing a serene approach. The benefits you will gain will speak for themselves."

58

Hassles

*W*ouldn't it be wonderful to live a life without hassles? A hassle-free existence would assure a life of serenity. Some people may be concerned that this would be boring. But this is not necessarily so. Your mind would be free to engage in many worthwhile pursuits.

Eliminating all hassles is not going to happen in the way the world works at present. So the next best thing is to eliminate the stress of hassles.

Expect hassles. No matter what you do, you will not be able to eliminate all hassles from your life. But you can learn to enjoy that which you previously viewed as a source of distress. Find amusement, enjoyment, and humor instead of frustration. Some people feel that it is not dignified for them to react in a light-hearted manner when faced with hassles. But it is a lot less dignified to react with stress and being upset.

You might find it helpful to ask yourself, "If I were in a highly creative frame of mind or a child who viewed this situation as a fun game, how would I react?"

I had often said, "I can't stand hassles." I used to blame hassles as being the source of my irritation. When it was suggested that I view hassles as a form of having fun, my reaction was, "Who are you kidding? They aren't fun and I don't want to fool myself."

The turning point was when I was a guest of my relative through marriage whom I hadn't seen in a long time. His brothers were also there and it was fascinating to see how they laughed while discussing various hassles they had experienced. They were all highly intelligent achievers. Their ability to laugh with regard to situations about which most people would have been upset has served as a model for me to emulate.

I asked my relative how they developed this pattern. He told me that his father and mother had always responded this way and they learned it from them. This can serve as an incentive for parents. Finding humor in their own hassles will be a great resource for their children.

59

The Challenge of Shyness

"How can I be serene when I'm so shy?" shy people often wonder. Even before you overcome your shyness, have a serene attitude toward being shy. There are many great people who were shy their entire lives. And many shy people accomplished a great deal. And there are many people who look totally outgoing and extroverted on the outside but inwardly they feel shy. And there are people who began life being shy and developed the thoughts and techniques that enabled them to overcome their shyness.

People who view themselves as shy usually repeat this self-concept over and over again. "Oh, I could never do what that person does, I'm too shy." "I can't ask people to buy what I would like to sell, I'm shy." "I've always found it difficult to speak up for myself, it's my nature to be shy." Stop viewing yourself as a person whose essence is shy. You have many more qualities that are a basic part of who you are. View yourself as someone who can say and do what needs to be said and done. And if right now this is not the real you, you can say, "I haven't yet mastered the skill of saying and doing whatever needs to be said and done and I'm working on acquiring this skill."

Accept the reality that you have a right to say and do things that are totally proper and right to do. It is just that shyness would hold you back. Then stop being so focused on how you feel and practice focusing on the other person or persons. How do they feel? What do they need? What could you say to them that would be kind? What can you say that will be an expression of care, concern, empathy, compassion, and just plain goodness? When you consistently practice this, you will become a master at feeling good around people. You will always make other people feel good and they will feel positive toward you. This is not people-pleasing in the negative sense, but gaining mastery over verbal kindness. You will be a truly kind person. You will be meeting the needs of others and engaging in character upgrading all the time.

Being naturally shy, I had to force myself to speak up in situations where most people appeared to me to be able to speak without giving the matter a second thought. I made it my goal to question three people each day about shyness. I realized that I would gain in two ways. Just interviewing many people would be initiating effective shyness-overcoming actions. And I was certain that I would hear many helpful ideas.

When I felt that someone never had an issue with shyness, I would say to them, "I have a tendency to be shy. It appears that you do not. Why aren't you shy?" In the beginning this was very difficult for me to ask. But they all seemed to feel complimented that I asked them. When someone seemed shy, I asked, "I have a problem with shyness. Can you share any ideas or tools that you find useful about asking people questions or taking action when at first it feels difficult?"

After a month of doing this, I felt transformed. I now felt that I could give many tips to others who could use it.

60
The Challenge of Change

It is easier to remain serene when everything remains the same. But in each person's life changes arise. At times these are minor and at times these can be major. The only way for one to be consistently serene is to be able to maintain serenity even when experiencing change. It is almost impossible to remain totally serene; nevertheless, coping with change calmly makes it much easier to handle.

Be prepared for change. Never assume that things will remain the same. Some people dread change. This makes it even harder for them. Not only do they suffer from changes when they actually occur, but just thinking about the possibility of a change puts them in an unresourceful state.

Whenever you think about a possible change, imagine yourself handling it calmly and peacefully. See yourself making the necessary moves with inner feelings of well-being. This might be a school change, a job change, a move to a different location, a financial change, a change in other people that affects you, and many other possibilities.

After a while every change becomes the normal way things are. The only question is how long it takes to adjust to the new situation. Serene people adjust quickly. Realize that you have already adjusted a multitude of times in your life. Just as in the past, you have succeeded in accepting new situations and circumstances, so too, you have the capacity to adjust to future changes. Each change you handle well becomes part of you, and makes it easier for you to cope with future changes.

I worked for a large company that had undergone many changes. When a number of my co-workers were told that they would have to look for new jobs, I began to panic. What would I do if I no longer had my main source of income?

I lost my appetite and could not sleep, I was so nervous. I observed that friends of mine reacted differently. Some were even more upset, even resentful. Others were calm. I spoke to the people who remained calm and began to learn from their strategies. These differed. Some made an effort to make themselves more valuable to the company. They made an effort to gain more knowledge and upgraded their skills. Others began to research alternative job opportunities. While they wanted to stay in the company, they prepared themselves to find a new job if necessary.

61

Conquering Envy

*E*nvy is a major factor that destroys one's life (*Ethics of the Fathers* 4:21). What is envy? It is feeling distressed because someone has more than you, knows more, has accomplished, or in any way is successful. We must eradicate envy in order to be serene. Envy robs one of happiness and peace of mind. Here are five concepts that will help you conquer envy.

(1) Have so much personal joy that, regardless of what anyone else has or does, you will still be happy and joyous. Build up a storehouse of gratitude for what you personally have. Be involved in meaningful positive actions that increase your joy.

(2) Realize that anything that might cause envy is an external factor. It is outside your brain. It is up to your perspective and frame how you will view the matter. Refuse to view it in a way that will needlessly cause you pain or distress.

(3) Use the "NEXT!" technique. If you happen to dwell on an envious thought, tell your brain, "NEXT!" and move on to more resourceful thoughts.

(4) Realize that the Almighty gives each person in this world exactly what he needs to fulfill his life's mission. If you do not have what someone else has it is because you do not need it to fulfill your life's purpose.

(5) Experience joy for the joy of others. Be happy for the success of other people. This is the quality that made Aaron worthy to be the High Priest. He was not jealous of his brother Moses being appointed the leader who would go to Pharaoh to demand that the Jewish nation be freed from slavery. Indeed, Aaron felt an inner joy for the success of his brother.

"Envy used to cause me intense pain," a joyous grandmother said. "When I was in school, I envied those students who received better grades, who were more popular, who had more money to spend. I envied my friends who married before I did. After I had children, I was envious of mothers who seemed to manage better than I did. Little by little, I came to the realization that it was up to me whether I would destroy my peace of mind with envious thoughts and feelings or not.

"Many of those who I envied had other difficulties and problems that I did not. I even heard some say that they envied me because I seemed so happy most of the time. Every once in a while envious thoughts enter my mind, but I have found it easier and easier to push them away and to focus on what I have and can appreciate.

62

Overconcern With Disapproval

*R*egardless of what you will do and how you will be, there will always be people who will be critical of you. You might have a limitation or pattern that will be looked upon negatively by others. To master serenity you need a balanced attitude.

Those who are overly concerned with the possibility of others being critical of them or not approving of them are likely to experience a lot of anxiety and stress. All the more so if someone actually says something negative. They will repeat the negative remarks over and over again in their minds and feel distress with each review. They may build up in their minds how awful this is and how much suffering this could cause them in the future. This is often an exaggeration.

To master serenity you need to take an objective view of the negativity of others. Perhaps there actually are actions and patterns that you should change and improve upon. But no matter what you do, there will always be those who see you in a negative light. If you can do something positive to improve this, by all means do so. When you cannot, let it go. This is a prerequisite for serenity mastery.

Your reaction to the disapproval of other people is up to you. We have frequently cited the example the Rambam offers of a righteous person who was asked about the happiest day of his life. It was when he was a passenger on a boat and others on board mocked and jeered him. They even threw trash at him. He was able to transcend their ridicule and not let this bother him. He felt joy when he saw how he had gained such mastery over his thoughts and feelings. Keep visualizing yourself reaching this level. It can take much mental practice. Freedom from fear of disapproval is so beneficial for serenity that it is a wise investment to work on this regardless of the effort involved.

I read about the prime minister of a small country who adopted policies that he felt was best for his people, but was criticized vehemently by his opponents. He never answered them. He would just state his position and ignored any negativity that was thrown his way. He would comment politely on what others said, but his whole manner showed that he did not allow put-downs or insults to affect him even slightly.

Someone commented about this: Really the words of others are harmless. They can only distress us if we allow them to. Create such an inner joy and empowerment that the negative noise of others is like the wind. You might find it helpful to repeat to yourself, "The more negative this person is the more intensely positive I will become."

63
Are You Nervous?
No!

It is common for people not to want others to think that they are nervous, worried, or anxious. They consider it very important to conceal this from everyone else. This can add to their anxiety. Not only do they feel the distress of their original feelings, they add to their distress by being overly concerned with what others who realize that they are nervous, worried, or anxious will think about them.

It is best to take a balanced approach. While it is not necessary to make anxiety and nervousness a favorite topic of discussion, in most instances one does not have to feel that it is terrible and awful if someone else realizes that one is nervous.

Prior to taking tests, job and school interviews, public speaking, difficult negotiations, and similar situations, it is normal to be slightly apprehensive and nervous. We are nervous because we want to succeed and feel that the upcoming challenge and our goal are important to us. Utilize this tension as power to do your best. Let this serve as a motivating factor to prepare adequately in advance. But do not feel a need to put on a brave face in order to prove that you are totally immune to normal human vulnerabilities.

If someone challenges you by saying, "You look nervous," do not feel that you need to deny it. It is preferable to respond with a simple, "Yes," or a cheery, "I certainly am." Taking a matter-of-fact attitude yourself is more admirable to most people than a denial that they know is not true.

The fear that others might see that you are not calm and relaxed is fear of an illusion. So what if someone thinks you are nervous? What do you actually lose? Those people are themselves almost certainly nervous on occasion. They may even feel a sense of relief to observe that others are like them and they too are not always serene.

Even if you are teaching a class on serenity, be open to the fact that you are not always serene. You may even be nervous about teaching that class. You may say, "I myself would love to be more serene and that is why I'm leading a discussion on these ideas."

Be sensitive to the need of others to conceal their nervousness or anxiety. Not everyone feels this need. But if someone does, you are doing an act of kindness by not bringing it up.

I was more anxious than most people about everyday living. It seemed to me that others were able to cope a lot better than I could in a wide range of things. "I don't want anyone to know how anxious I am" was a sentence that frequently reverberated in my mind.

Someone who realized how much of an effort I made to conceal my anxiety challenged me about this.

"Why is it so bad if others know that you are nervous?" he asked me.

'Then they will think that I'm not normal," I replied.

"What's not normal about being nervous? I think it's not normal to be always cool, calm, and collected. Very few people have totally mastered being serene and perfectly calm and relaxed in all situations. If anything, they will think you are normal when they see that you are nervous."

"But I'm more nervous than most people," I argued.

"Perhaps, that's so," he said. "But if you are calm and lighthearted about being nervous, many people will respect that and admire you for this ability."

'I never thought about this that way," I said. Since that conversation, I have no longer considered it so important to hide my anxiety. This gave me a great feeling of relief and helped me decrease my total stress level.

64

The Kindness of Increasing Serenity

elping people become more serene is a great act of kindness. By becoming knowledgeable of what is helpful, you will be doing a wonderful service for others.

The first principle in helping people is: Give hope. Actually the first principle is: Do not make them feel worse. But we already mentioned this. Believe that serenity is a learnable skill that everyone can master and you will be able to pass along this awareness to those who are not yet serene.

What has worked for you to help you become more serene when you have been in distressful states? This may be helpful to the specific individual you are trying to help and then again it may not be. Everyone is different. This may be a good starting place, but be aware of the feedback, often nonverbal, to ascertain if you are on the right track.

For many people, just having an opportunity to talk to someone about their thoughts and feelings can help alleviate distressful feelings. By being an understanding and empathetic listener, you will be helping them greatly.

You may ask the people you are trying to help, "What has helped you be serene in the past?" They may say something that is applicable in their present situation. Or they may say, "I was able to be serene before because my life situation was different." Or, "I was serene in this tranquil garden, but I find it difficult to be serene where I am now." These are valid points. Nevertheless, what they tell you can give you insight as to what might be helpful for them now.

Some people may like to hear ideas conducive to serenity. Others may prefer tools and techniques. Some may appreciate being reminded to breathe slowly and deeply. You can suggest that they repeat, "With every breath I take I'm becoming calmer and calmer." Try this yourself first. When you experience that this works for you, you will be able to "sell" this to others more effectively.

I am extremely grateful to a friend who has taught me how to be serene. I used to suffer a lot from anxiety and stress. Externally my life didn't seem that rough, but internally I was a nervous wreck. I was totally miserable. I had studied various approaches for accessing calm and relaxed states, but I rarely remembered to access them on my own when I need them the most. A friend considers it one of his main goals to serve as a coach to calm me down and help me learn to be serene. For over two months he would call me at least four times each day. He would ask about the states I wanted for myself. He would ask me how I felt and what I said to myself and visualized when I was in those states. When I expressed my depth of gratitude, he told me that the best thing I could do for him was to similarly serve as a coach to someone else. If people knew how grateful I am to one who helps me escape from mental torture into mental freedom, they would greatly cherish the opportunity to help others like this friend helped me.

65

Do It Right

$\mathcal{J}$t is a great act of kindness to help others decrease their stress, tension, nervousness, frustration, and worry, and increase feelings of serenity. But there is a right way and a wrong way of doing this. It is preferable to refrain from saying anything to someone about their emotional states than to say things that will just increase their level of stress.

A well-known principle in communication that we often repeat is: The meaning of your communication is dependent on the results that you get. If what you say makes someone calmer and more serene, then what you have said is kind and helpful. And if it makes someone feel worse, that communication is counterproductive.

What shouldn't you say? Anything that implies a put-down. Here are some notorious examples:

"You seem nervous today. Calm down."

"What's wrong with you? You're always stressed out."

"Don't be a baby. Anyone should be able to handle this."

"You're overreacting."

"You're supposed to be a religious person. You should have more trust. It's not fitting for you to be worried and nervous."

"You certainly won't get any prizes for excelling at serenity."

If you have already caused someone distress by saying the wrong things, apologize. You may say something along these lines: "I'm sorry that I was insensitive earlier. When I'm honest with myself, I realize that I, too, experience more stress and anxiety than I like to acknowledge. I am committed to being more sensitive in the future."

I tend to be highly anxious. One of the worst things about this is that other people keep trying to be helpful in unhelpful ways. I asked someone for ideas on how to handle this. He suggested that I say, "That wasn't helpful," if someone was totally insensitive. If someone truly tried to be helpful but wasn't, I could say, "I thank you for your good intentions. What I really need is understanding and not suggestions." And if I would prefer that someone not say anything, I should increase my state of courage and respectfully say, "I appreciate that you want to be helpful to me. And what I find most helpful is for people to refrain from saying anything. I consider it an act of kindness to just let me be. Thank you for caring."

66

Help Others Help You

*T*here are people who would be more than willing to help you become more serene if they knew what to say that would be helpful. Help them help you.

Some people might not say anything because they do not want to say the wrong things and are concerned that you may become irritated or angry with them for their input. You may miss out on their assistance. If you let them know what would be appreciated, they will gladly say it. But they are not mind readers and do not know your inner thoughts. Tell them what it is you want them to say.

This is especially important with those who try to help you become less anxious, worried, nervous, frustrated, etc., but say the wrong things. Instead of helping you become more serene, their words make you feel worse. If you do not suggest what you would appreciate and you are able to do so, you are a partner in their counterproductive approach. It may not be your fault. You did not think of telling them what you want. For that same reason it is not their fault either; they do not spitefully say the wrong thing, they just have not yet learned what the right thing is. Give them the guidance they need.

Think about what has helped you become more serene in the past. What have people said to you that you appreciated? What was the gist of what they said? What was their tone of voice?

You may find it helpful if someone says, "What state would you like to be in right now? When have you been in that state before? What can you tell yourself or do to access that state now?" For some people like myself this will be helpful if said in an objective tone of voice. Said sarcastically, it will not have the proper effect. Other people would not want anyone saying this to them. They do not even like saying this to themselves.

Only you can know exactly what you want. But you may feel differently on different days. On some days, one thing would be exactly what you would like to hear. On other days, you just want to be left alone. Thank people for trying and give them feedback on what would be useful.

Focus on what they can do and what you would want. Do not just tell them that whatever they are doing is wrong. If you do not know what you do want and only know what you do not want, tell them. You could say, "I would love to tell you what would be beneficial for me. But at this moment I don't exactly know. I will gladly give you suggestions as soon as I think of what might work."

Whenever someone tells you something that helped you become calmer, more centered, or more serene, make a mental or written note of it. Then you can ask other friends and relatives to try this out.

If you know what would be helpful, why would you need someone else to say it to you? Some people do not. But many others will find that when they are stressed or anxious, the calm and serene voice of someone else has a soothing effect on their states. They themselves know what to say, but being in an unresourceful state themselves they are not able to help themselves as much as someone else can.

Some individuals would really want to tell others to say something calming or soothing, but they feel shy or reluctant to ask others for help. This is a time to access one's courage state. Remember what it is like to be totally courageous. Think of a courageous role model and imagine being that person. Let your courageous part speak for you. Visualize yourself being in a courageous state. The benefits of asking are great enough to outweigh the drawbacks of not asking.

Can you ask everyone? Of course not. But kind people will cherish the opportunity to help another human being. Do not deprive them of this opportunity.

67

Partners in Serenity Mastery

*V*iew each person who irritates you, provokes you, intimidates you, or distresses you as your partner in mastering serenity. If no one at all is around, you might be serene, but you still have not become a master of serenity. For this you need partners.

When someone says or does something that sets you off balance, it is easy to view that person in a negative light. The more negative your view, the more power you give that person to cause you distress. You may blame him or her, but you are a partner in causing your own distress. If you do not allow yourself to participate in "the dance of distress," you will remain in a calmer state. It takes your mental participation with that person to create a lack of serenity. If you could totally ignore that person's way of talking or acting, you would not have a stressful reaction. Often this is neither possible nor advisable. But understanding how your own participation helps create your reaction gives you greater power to control your own reaction.

When you are able to maintain serenity in the face of provocation, you are creating a serenity-building partnership with that other person. Remaining serene now makes serenity an increased integral part of your being. And you could only have done this with your partner's assistance. You might still wish that this person would no longer challenge you. But wishes do not create reality. Since this person is seeing or doing something, he is automatically a partner in your reaction. You are the one who chooses whether this will be a distressful partnership or one that builds greater serenity.

Think of any people you might have viewed in the past as being the cause of your not being as serene as you would have wished. From now on utilize the opportunities these people give you to develop an unshakable serenity. It is those who challenge you the most who will be your most effective teachers.

One particular relative was a constant source of irritation for me. We argued and quarreled and said things to each other that we both regretted. I viewed him as being a difficult person and at times abusive. This made me even angrier at some of the things he said or failed to say, did or failed to do.

It was suggested that I view him as my serenity-building partner. Right away I felt a profound change. My new perspective helped me remain calmer. By remaining calm, what I said and the way I said it was far more pleasant. This created a positive loop. In a relatively short while, the difficult person disappeared and in his place was someone with whom I actually enjoyed interacting.

68
Wait Until You Are Serene

There are many situations when it is preferable to wait until you are serene before interacting with another person. You may need to influence someone to do or not do something, you may need to work out a misunderstanding or a dispute, you may need to calm someone down, or you may need to ask someone for a favor. Your own emotional state will influence the other person's state and will influence what you say and how you say it.

How long will it take you to become serene? This obviously will depend on many factors unique to the specific situation, your general personality, and your mastery of your states. At times you may access a serene state in a few moments. At other times it might take a while, even a day or two. When something is important for you to be at your best, it is worth waiting until you are able to utilize the inner resources that are yours when you are serene.

Many people would theoretically agree that it is often preferable for them to wait until they are in a serene state. The issue is that they forget to be aware about their state. Only later do they look back and realize that they should have waited to speak or act until after they were calmer and more relaxed and could think more clearly. The solution is to make it a habit to automatically think about your state whenever you are faced with a difficult encounter.

A question to habitually ask yourself is: "What is the best state for right now?" At times this will be serenity and at times other states. The benefit of this question is that it is all purposeful. Once you are aware that you want to be serene right now, you can: Act, breath, and speak the way you are when you are serene. Remember times and moments when you have already been serene. Mirror and model serene people. Use creative imagery conducive for serenity together with serene autosuggestion.

At times you may be in a resourceful state, but the person you need to interact with is not. When you personally can say something that will improve his state, great. If you do not feel that you can right now, it is often wise to wait a while until the other person's state is more conducive for a better interaction.

"I tend to be very emotional," a highly successful influencer of people said. "This is my biggest strength and also my biggest vulnerability. When I feel positive about something, I feel this strongly and am able to communicate my positive feelings. But when I am upset, I also feel this strongly. It took me a long time

to realize that it's a high priority for me to be calm and centered before speaking to someone about highly charged matters. A number of times I have strongly regretted the way I spoke when I was angry. The time it takes for me to access a serene state before speaking is much more preferable than rushing and saying the wrong things.

"As a professional communicator, I consider this one of the biggest mistakes people make when communicating. They try to get their points across before they are in a centered and focused state. The first rule of communication is to access a resourceful state before you speak."

69

"It's Not My Nature"

$\mathcal{S}$ ome people argue, "It's not my nature to be serene." Since they view serenity as impossible for them, their mistaken viewpoint becomes their reality. And since they are rarely serene, it helps them "prove" that they just do not have a serene gene.

Serenity is created by the patterns we form in our minds. And stress is created by mentally forming different patterns. It is the nature of human minds and bodies to create the emotional states that are consistent with the specific pattern that is being formed by one's brain at a given moment. Brains that form thought patterns of gratitude and celebration naturally create happiness and joy. Brains that dwell on thought patterns of pessimism, negativity, discontent, and discouragement naturally create sadness and depression. Brains that dwell on thought patterns of tranquility, harmony, and soothing messages naturally create serenity. So it is not one's "nature" that does or does not create serenity, but one's pattern of thought.

Once you believe wholeheartedly that it is within your capability to be serene, you will find yourself being serene more and more often. And this will make it even easier for you to believe that your nature includes serenity.

"I've never been serene, and I don't think I ever will be," the busy executive claimed.

"It's a skill that you can learn," he was told.

"Not me," he said. "It's just not my nature."

"If it were something you could learn, would you practice until you've mastered it?" he was challenged.

After agreeing to try, this is what was said to him, "Your brain has a standard waking state that is called a beta state. This is usually a frequency of twenty cycles per second. When you slow it down to between fourteen and seven cycles per second, this state is called an alpha state. At the alpha state, you experience serenity and your brain is more open to suggestions. An easy way to access this state is to close your eyelids and slightly raise your eyeballs as if you were watching something on a large screen. In this state, suggest to yourself, 'I will relax all of my muscles from head to toe. My entire being will be calm, relaxed, and serene.' Practice this frequently. When you do this often enough, you will increase your ability to access this serene state whenever you wish. After doing this properly, you will be totally convinced that it is in your nature to be serene. You just need to apply the appropriate patterns."

70

"*If*…"

"*I* would be more serene if…" is a common phrase that describes the pattern used as an excuse for not being serene.

- "I would be more serene if every person I interacted with would be respectful, considerate, and serene."
- "I would be more serene if life were easier."
- "I would be more serene if I wouldn't have any problems."
- "I would be more serene if everyone would do what I ask them to do right away."
- "I would be more serene if things would always work out the way that I wanted them to."

This is true for everyone. We all would be serene if life were easy, every person we interact with would be respectful, considerate, and serene, we would not have any problems, everyone would do what we ask them to do right away, and things would always work out the way we wanted them to. But it is quite obvious that this is not the way life on this planet actually happens.

The way to create serenity for yourself given that things are the way they are and not the way we would always wish, the big "If" of serenity is: "You will be serene if you consistently create serenity in your mind."

Wishing for the impossible will not help you become more serene. Creating a mental mindset of serenity even though the external environment is not perfect will.

"Of course I'm not serene," I would tell everyone who asked me why I was so stressed out. "How could anyone be serene if so many things were going wrong?"

"What would you need to happen to be serene?" my Rabbi asked me.

I gave him my list. It was quite long.

"How long do you feel that you will have to wait until this becomes reality?" my Rabbi asked me with a smile.

I had to acknowledge that it was highly unlikely that all the factors on my list would even be in perfect alignment.

"Increase your level of gratitude for all that you can be grateful for," my Rabbi said. "There will always be reasons why you can't be happy or serene. By keeping your focus on the positive factors and doing what you can to change what can be changed, you will be much more serene than if you kept your focus on your reasons for not being serene."

This advice has helped me tremendously and I often repeat it to others.

71

The Ostrich Approach

*S*ome people feel that the only way they can remain calm is to deny reality. They are like the proverbial ostrich that sticks its head in the sand when troubles arise. If it cannot see the danger, it assumes that the damage no longer exists. The problem with this approach is that ignoring danger does not make it disappear. In fact, not being aware of the present reality or the potential difficulties that may arise prevents you from doing all you can to actually protect yourself.

What are the qualities and inner resources that will enable a person to face life's challenges without denying them? Courage is one. Serene empowerment is another. Both together are powerful.

Visualize yourself experiencing a serene sense of your ability to cope with whatever arises. Some people are concerned that this might be negative thinking. But negative thinking is when you experience anxiety in the present because you are concerned that you will not be able to cope well with challenges that have yet to arise. When you mentally build up your inner strength and courage to cope well with all eventualities, your character keeps developing. You are building up your inner resources and will be stronger for doing so.

An acquaintance recently told me that he was too frightened to tell others that he was afraid of things going wrong. In the home he grew up in, if anyone ever expressed a worry or concern about some problem arising, he was scolded and rebuked. "Don't be so negative," he was told. "Be positive and all will be just fine."

Being rebuked for sharing his thoughts made him keep them to himself. But they didn't disappear. He had to act as if he wasn't worried about anything even when he felt an intense need to express his thoughts to others. This resulted in muscle tension and physical pain. He went to a doctor for medication to ease the pain. After asking many questions, the doctor told him that any medicine would only be a Band-Aid. What he really needed was to talk about what truly bothered him. Then he could work on finding tools to cope. But even before any of these tools helped, acknowledging to someone that he was worried would lighten his burden.

"When I was growing up, my parents told me that I shouldn't worry," he said. "I should just assume that everything will work out all right."

"If you really felt that way, you wouldn't be having these tension pains," the doctor told him. "You need to find a good

listener who will be willing to hear about your worries. Then you can analyze them and see what you can do on a practical level. When you acknowledge your worries, you build up more courage to handle them."

72

Always?

$\mathscr{I}$ have often been asked, "I want to be serene always. How can I be certain that I will be serene all the time?"

I personally do not think that this is a wise way to word a goal. As soon as one is nervous, frustrated, anxious, upset, irritated, worried, or angry for even a few moments, he is not in a serene state during that time. Even very great people experience these states; if not for trivial matters, then out of their concern for the welfare of others for whom they care.

If someone makes it his goal to be "always serene," he is likely to keep his focus on all the moments when he is not serene. Since his goal is not just to increase his level of serenity, but to be serene nonstop, every moment of not being serene is an automatic negation of his goal. For the vast majority of human beings, the goal of always being serene will be impossible to reach. Setting impossible goals can be frustrating — unless one has a totally serene attitude about not reaching one's goals.

As we have previously stated, if you make it your goal to be able to access serenity at will, then at any given moment you can reach your goal by accessing serenity that moment. This goal is reachable, since you need not be serene absolutely all the time. All you need to do is be serene in a present moment, and then you can rejoice that you are building up your skill of creating serenity for yourself. Each and every moment of serenity is an accomplishment of your goal.

My teachers spoke often about the importance of consistency. I felt that this was a wonderful goal. But as a strongly emotional 18-year-old, I found myself frequently in a state of frustration. At times I felt totally discouraged.

The first question I would ask new teachers was, "What can I do to ensure that I will always be consistent?"

The person who helped me the most suggested that I change the goal. My goal should be to be the master of my thoughts, feelings (also known as states), words, and actions one moment at a time. When I keep this up, then I will be consistent. If I lose it, then I should immediately regain mastery of my thoughts, states, words, and actions. If my goal were just to be consistent, then I may feel like a failure and be tempted to give up. With the new wording of my goal, I will feel more and more empowered as time goes on.

73

Had I Known ...

"*H*ad I known about this traffic jam, I would have taken the other route.*"

"Had I known that a new and upgraded version of this would be out so soon, I would have waited to make my purchase."

"Had I known that I could have bought this at a lower price in a different section of the city, I would have gone there."

"Had I known that the person wouldn't be home when I knocked on his door, I would have gone elsewhere."

We all know much more after the fact than before. In hindsight we all see more comprehensively. To keep rehashing what we would have done if we would have known things that we did not or could not have known simply adds to one's stress.

Awareness of *hashgachah pratis*, Divine Providence, creates serenity. We went where we did, for a purpose. We made the purchase when we did, for a purpose. Things took longer than we thought they would, for a purpose. Learn from each experience, but do not spend time regretting your actions when you did not do anything wrong.

Every situation helps you develop your character. You gain humility from every instance when you realize that you are a fallible human being and are not omniscient. And every situation is yet another opportunity to be serene even when it is a challenge to be so.

A visit to an old-age home taught me an important lesson about how futile it is to keep regretting past choices over and over again. The eighty-year-old man was in relatively good health and very polite. But people avoided him. His only topic was, "I should have ..." He would talk at length how he should have bought or sold this or that property. He should have traveled here or there. He should have invested in this or that stock. He should have accomplished more, read more, learned more skills, and on and on he went. An hour of this nonstop regret about what he could have and should have left me with a super-heavy feeling. I could barely imagine what his life was like. He had to hear this inner chatter all the time.

Then I realized that I, also, engage in this too frequently. Not as much as he did, but still way too often. I was totally committed to make the most of my present moments instead of wasting time and energy on what is over and done with.

74

Beyond Your Control

*T*hings that cause you stress fall into two categories: those that you can control and those that are beyond your control. Serene people are able to focus on accomplishing and changing what they can. This keeps their mind involved with constructive matters and frees them from focusing on what they cannot control. We were not put into this world to do the impossible. Those who tend to take positive action do not spend the major part of their energy on being upset about matters which they cannot do anything to change.

There are many borderline issues. "Perhaps this is a situation that I can do something about, perhaps not. Maybe I can speak to someone who can give me ideas about what I can do, maybe not. Possibly if I think more about this, I will come up with a creative idea that I hadn't thought about previously, possibly not." There are no definitive rules and axioms that will let us know what is under our control and what is not. The world has had many people who bravely and persistently kept seeking solutions and inventions that others had considered beyond the realm of possibility.

From the perspective of serenity, develop a calm attitude toward trying to resolve issues that are under question. Accept the fact that even if you spend an extremely large amount of time trying, you might not find a solution. The time you spent doing this was an effort to find a solution. Without trying as you did, you would have no way of knowing that you would not find a solution. The mental effort you put into this may bear fruit later on. It will make you more aware of what to look for when you speak to other people or read articles on the topic. Perhaps at the present the solution does not yet exist, but it could be found in a week or two, a year or two, even a decade or two.

Pray for guidance and wisdom. Pray for the Almighty's help in situations when you yourself cannot do anything to change a situation. Prayer helps you realize that even when you can say and do things to improve a situation, it is the Almighty's assistance that makes it happen. Pray for the inner strength to cope with all that you need to cope with. And pray for serenity both in situations that are within your control and those that are not.

Regardless of what is beyond your control, your attitude toward your situation and circumstances are within your control. Some people have a greater amount of control over this and some less. The more effort you put into mastery of your mental focus and your ability to reframe and reframe positively and resourcefully, the easier it will be for you to master a serene focus and attitude even in the most difficult situations.

"I was always able to handle the daily events of my personal life quite well. It's the situations that are in the news, as it were, that would cause a lot of stress and anxiety. Stories about violence and car accidents, poverty and suffering, tragedies and disasters, these are what I found difficult to handle. Some people have told me that I should try to avoid hearing about these sorts of things. But I felt that this would be callous and a lack of concern for humanity even though I knew that I couldn't do anything to change matters.

"I discussed this with a teacher of mine and he said, 'Caring about the welfare of others is an elevating quality. This is the quality that made Moses the great leader that he was. Great people throughout all the generations had this quality. Make it your goal to maintain a realistic balance. The distress you feel for the anguish of others is an elevating quality. This perspective will give you the strength to process this and at the same time come back to a mental place of serenity as a general state of being. This isn't easy, but it's a goal to strive for.'

"Having made this my goal has enabled me to be aware of what is happening to other people and still live my life with a general feeling of well-being and serenity."

75

Being at Ease in Every Situation

$\mathcal{A}$ master of total serenity will be at ease in every situation. Most of us are not at this level of mastery. I am not and neither are the vast majority of people I have spoken with about serenity. Make it your goal to increase the number of situations where you will be at ease.

Each person has situations where he feels at ease and other situations where he feels uncomfortable. When you personally feel at ease, how do you do it? What is your attitude toward yourself? What is your attitude toward the other individual, group, or crowd? How do you view the situation itself? Compare this with how you view yourself, others, and the situation when you do not feel at ease. This will indicate where your starting point is and where you want to go mentally to upgrade your ability to be more at ease in more situations.

Think of a role model who feels at ease in situations when you do not. Imagine that you are that person. You might want to imagine trying on, as it were, that person's head to think in the way that person thinks, and to feel the inner calm and self-assurance that this person generally projects.

No one on the planet Earth has been given special privileges to feel at ease. It is always an individual's choice. You, too, can make this choice. Yes, some people find this easier than others and some children do this quite naturally. But everyone can improve their skill in this area. Just being cognizant that it is a skill makes it easier.

In a situation where you do not feel at ease, mentally visualize yourself becoming more serene with each breath you take. As you exhale, feel the tension leaving. As you inhale, feel yourself becoming more and more serene. When you realize that you are becoming even a little more serene than when you began, feel great that you are making progress. This will make it even easier to continue along your path of being at ease in more and more situations.

I used to be very self-conscious when I was in a group. I felt this most strongly when I entered a room full of strangers or when a class or meeting had already started. I made it my goal to feel more comfortable in these situations.

I used my imagination to visualize that everyone greeted me with a friendly smile and wave of their hand. I imagined that they were all happy to see me. I knew that if this were the reality, it would be simple for me to feel at ease. By mentally projecting positive feelings toward others, I knew that they would be likely to reciprocate. While I'm still not a total master, the progress I've made so far is beyond what I had thought possible for myself.

76

Learning New Skills

*W*hen you are beginning to learn a new skill, what is your emotional response? Some people become exceedingly nervous. They do not yet know what to do. Even if they already know the basics, they are not proficient. What will other people think of them if they do not catch on right away? They might self-judge themselves negatively if it takes them longer than others to learn the skill.

Those who are calm and relaxed when learning a new skill utilize their brain at its optimal level. Anxiety and stress prevents one's brain from doing all it can do. By remaining serene, your brain takes in more information quicker. Even if in the past your pattern has been to become nervous when trying to learn a new skill, right now you have the ability to learn the skill of being serene when learning new skills. And you can choose to do this serenely.

When you are calm, your brain automatically takes in all that it sees and hears. Even if you are not yet able to have total recall of what you saw and heard, it is stored in the library of your brain. When you wish to access that information, being serene helps you do so more readily.

People differ in how many times they need something repeated. Each of us differs in how we take in information depending on several factors, which include: when we have a natural talent for something and when we do not, when we are highly motivated to learn a specific skill and when we are not, and when we are in our best learning states and when we are in our least. Even in the worst-case scenario, when you are serene you will do much better than when you are not.

So when you want to learn a new skill, mentally prepare yourself. Breathe slowly and deeply a number of times. Tell yourself, "Now I am going to allow myself to be totally calm and relaxed. I am feeling more and more serene with each breath." Then imagine that your brain is a video camera. Watch what others who have that skill say and do. Your brain records it all. Read the instructions serenely. Realize that as you are reading, your magnificent brain absorbs all that you see. When you need to recall the information, access a serene state. When you make mistakes, realize that your brain is upgrading your level of expertise by mentally filing what not to do and what needs to be done.

I became so nervous when I tried to learn new skills that I decided that I was limited in what I could learn. Someone who offered courses in gaining certain skills saw that I was resistant to taking a course from which I would gain a great deal. "What is the real reason why you are hesitant?" he asked me.

"I feel very uncomfortable when I try to learn new things like this," I admitted to him.

"What thoughts go through your mind as you try to listen?" he asked.

"I'm not certain," I replied.

"For the next few days recall situations when you tried to learn new skills. Be aware of all the thoughts that run through your mind," he suggested.

I found it highly informative to see that instead of paying attention to what someone was trying to teach me, I kept repeating insecure thoughts that blocked my ability to take in what was being said. I was resolved to quiet my mind when I listened to instructions. This was the solution that enabled me to enjoy learning new skills.

77

Serenity at Work

*W*ork can be a major source of stress for many people. There is the work itself. There are often issues which involve varying conditions. The pay may not be enough, the hours may be too long, too much travel, the job may be boring, supervisors or other employees may be challenging, changes may necessitate learning new skills, and then there is always the possibility of losing one's job.

Regardless of difficulties at work, whether or not one will be able to maintain serenity is up to one's own mind. Having work to do is obviously better than needing the money and not having a job. Make it a priority to continue to develop your level of serenity at work. When you are able to access a serene state at will, you will be free from much stress. A challenging job itself will be part of your comprehensive plan to master serenity.

When you are in a serene state, you will problem-solve more effectively. You will find it easier to improve conditions. At times a minor change can make a major difference.

When you are serene, you can analyze the entire situation and decide if it is in your best interests to stay or to change jobs. When you are objective, you will be aware that every job has its advantages and disadvantages. When you are serene, you will not make an impulsive decision to leave when that would not be wise. Just by being more serene, the same job will go more smoothly.

A fellow who was earning a fantastic salary at a large company told me that over the years he thought of quitting a number of times. As he was working his way up, the grass always seemed greener elsewhere.

A number of people who had left the company over the years had basically told him, "It's not worth doing this job. The stress is just too great."

He agreed. It was not worth dying for the job. So he was resolved to remain calm and relaxed at work. He realized that while some stress is almost inevitable, he would eliminate most of it by developing a calm attitude. What helped him was meeting a serene 87-year-old man in good health. "Trivial things aren't worth getting upset about," the man told him, "and most things are trivial." This became his motto also. His serenity at work helped him in his personal life also and his entire family gained.

78

Anxiety and Panic Attacks

*G*eneralized anxiety and panic attacks are at the opposite end of the spectrum from serenity. Anxiety is the body's reaction to danger. When one is truly in danger, the anxiety is a warning signal to get out of harm's way. When someone is in actual danger, such as a close call with a speeding car or an object falling from a roof, as soon as the danger has passed, the body begins the process of getting back to normal. Milder cases of anxiety can occur prior to tests, to challenging encounters, to speaking in public, and other situations where we feel nervous. These are normal and almost everybody will experience them in various situations.

At times anxiety is caused by physical disorders such as hyperthyroidism and hypoglycemia. At other times it can be caused by substance intoxications such as caffeine. Panic attacks that appear spontaneously without a valid cause can be mild or severe. What is happening is that the body is going in a fight or flight syndrome without an actual threat.

Remaining as calm as possible under the circumstances and trying to understand what is happening physiologically can take away some of the feelings that occur during a panic attack. Typical symptoms of panic are: one's heart pounds; one breathes faster than usual; one has chest pains; one's legs might feel rubbery. There can be feelings of dissociation, bright light can be disturbing; there is sweating; numbness of the hands; tingling in the mouth; a choking sensation; and trembling, which may be accompanied by a feeling that one is having a heart attack, that one may be going crazy or dying. The terror that some people experience makes them even more anxious than would be caused just by the bodily symptoms. Because this is so distressing, many people who experience this have a fear that these feelings will recur. And this causes anxiety even when there are not any of the symptoms at the onset.

The symptoms are caused by the heart speeding up to transport blood and oxygen; one breathes faster to obtain more oxygen for the muscles; muscles tighten and this causes chest pain; there is blood supply buildup in the legs and decreased oxygen to the brain. Pupils dilate for more acute vision and therefore bright lights are disturbing. There is numbness in the hands due to the diversion of blood to the muscles. The tingling in one's mouth is caused by hyperventilating. The shaking and choking sensation is due to increased muscle tension. These physiological reactions are beneficial in helping one to flee from danger or, if necessary, to stand firm and fight to save his life.

By breathing slowly and calmly, you will be helping the body return to a more normal state. As you breathe slowly and deeply, slowly speak to yourself in calming ways. ("Calm and relaxed. Calm and relaxed.") If you can be immersed in your body's sensations, you will be forestalling the added anxiety that would be caused by fear.

Keep in mind that the goal is to get one's muscles to relax. By definition, when a person who has experienced the tensing of muscles which we label "panic attack" relaxes those muscles, the anxiety has passed. When one's muscles become very relaxed and one's mind is at peace, one is in the state of serenity. Knowing your goal is a vital step toward reaching it.

It is worthwhile for those who experience panic attacks or generalized anxiety to consult a competent health professional who specializes in anxiety. There are many approaches and if an approach does not seem to be the right one for you, consult another professional.

Be sensitive to the distress of someone going through a panic attack. The suffering is real. Empathetic listening to what the sufferer has to say can have a calming effect. People who have not personally experienced anxiety attacks may not realize how distressful they are. Just being aware of this can help you be more understanding.

79

Stress Breeds Mistakes

*W*hen you are under stress, your brain functions at diminished levels of efficiency. Therefore it is easy to make mistakes. When under heightened levels of stress, it is easy to make decisions which are not beneficial. During negotiations, when under stress, it is easy to acquiesce to something that you will subsequently regret.

Decrease your level of stress and increase your level of serenity before coming to a decision such as conceding in a negotiation. If someone tries to rush you, you have the right and the ability to calm yourself first in order to think more clearly.

If you are not able to wait for another day, at least wait a few minutes to calm down. Walk around. Drink some water. Breathe slowly and deeply. Mentally access a calm, relaxing scene for a few minutes. In the vast majority of instances you have the option of remaining silent for a few minutes. Do not allow others to rush you into a deal that would be detrimental for you. View this pressure as an unfair tactic. It is very possible that the other person does not have any evil intent in pressuring you to arrive at a decision. He may have a personal need to come to an immediate agreement. It could be that he is just impatient without a strong and valid reason. That is just the way he is. You might find it helpful to say to yourself, "The more this person tries to rush me, the more patient and serene I will become."

I attended a seminar given by an internationally successful lawyer who was a world-class expert negotiator. His services were utilized by presidents of the United States, by the leaders of other countries, and by giant corporations.

"I don't negotiate for myself," he acknowledged. "When I'm emotionally involved, I make mistakes. Do I have self-esteem? Tremendous self-esteem. Great levels of confidence. Comprehensive knowledge of the art of negotiation. Yet when I am under stress, I make stupid mistakes. And what is true for me is true for everyone else also."

Keep this in mind whenever you are about to negotiate for yourself. What is the solution: "Care. But don't care too much about the outcome. Excessive stress is a proven prescription for failure."

80

Feeling Different

Feeling that one is different from others can be a constant source of distress. Individuals may feel this way for a wide variety of reasons. Some because they do not speak the spoken language fluently. Their mother tongue is different, and they speak with a noticeable accent. It may be because someone looks different in some way. Some people are not as scholarly or as knowledgeable in specific areas. There are multiple reasons why someone might feel different.

The reality is that every single human is unique and everyone is different than everyone else; it is just a matter of degree. So if someone will create a lack of serenity because of being different, every single person alive now, or who has lived in the past, and all those who will eventually live have a reason for not being serene. Even if one is very similar to other people in one's immediate environment, there are many other environments which are highly dissimilar.

Being different can be an objective reality. But there is no law of the universe that this has to cause a lack of serenity. If even one person in the world is serene, that means one can be different and be serene. That person must be different in many ways from every other person. He has a unique genetic nature, a unique tone of voice, a unique look, a unique life history, a unique way of looking at things, unique fingerprints, and many other unique distinctions.

Mentally accept that you are an integral part of the world. Each human being has intrinsic worth and value, regardless of how similar or different he is from anyone else. In most instances differences are neither good nor bad, simply different. As we have repeated many times, how you feel about this depends on how you personally and subjectively view it. Do not view this as a problem and it is not. When you project sincere positive feelings toward others, they will feel positive toward you. Keep your focus on this and you will find it easier to maintain serenity even though you are different.

I grew up in a small town and even though I lived in a large city for many years, I always felt a bit awkward. My accent was different, and my conversation did not flow as easily as most of the people I encountered daily. This was a constant source of anxiety for me. I tried to be more like everyone else, but no matter how hard I tried I still felt very different.

I shared my inner feelings with an understanding teacher. He told me that he too felt different — at times very different and at times just slightly different. What helped him was that he decided that mentally he would bless people and wish them well. Whenever he could do an act of kindness for someone, he went out of his way to do so. He projected such positive energy that others reciprocated. He felt that others liked him in return and the fact that he was different did not really make a difference in the way they treated him. After this discussion I put my main focus on mentally blessing people and doing acts of kindness, my concerns about being different disappeared and my level of serenity increased.

81

Losing Money

*M*oney dealings and our reactions in situations which involve money reveals a lot about who we are. The Talmud considers this one of the three basic ways that the character and personality of someone can be recognized. (Anger and how one reacts when under the influence of alcohol are the other two.)

In order to master serenity one must be able to face financial losses and challenges serenely. First recognize where your personal challenges are when it comes to money. Are you nervous regarding having enough money for basic necessities or are you certain that you will always be able to have what you need? How generous are you? In what ways does money enhance your life and in what ways does money cause you problems? Being upset over the loss of money can be a source of considerable distress.

It is a very high spiritual level to be able to maintain serenity in the face of a major financial loss. Right now what we are addressing is losing serenity over minor, inconsequential amounts.

Money is not a goal in and of itself. It is a means to an end. With money we purchase items that we feel will enhance our lives. One of the major reasons people want more money than they presently need is in order to have peace of mind.

But money itself cannot guarantee peace of mind. In fact, the more money someone has the more potential there is to find things to worry about. No matter how much money one possesses, it takes mastery over one's thoughts to be consistently serene.

At least when it comes to minor financial setbacks remember that losing serenity is a far greater loss. Just as you would take care not to repeat a ridiculous mistake that caused a loss of a dollar or two, so too, be careful not to repeat mistakes that cause you to lose serenity.

A question that is a helpful tool is, "Will this loss cause me a practical, noticeable loss?" Whenever the answer is, "No," learn from the experience and come back to a serene state. By mastering the ability to do this with small amounts one will be able to remain calmer and more centered even when large amounts are involved.

I was able to handle significant losses with confidence and a positive attitude. My father was a successful businessman and he used to say, "Some days you make a large profit and some days you lose. In the end it works out." Profits and losses are an integral part of every businessman's life. But I used to become very angry if someone overcharged me even a small amount.

*"How much is it worth for you to be consistently joyous?"
I was asked by someone who cared about me. He went on to
explain to me that I should view minor losses as the price I
will be paying to master serenity. Investing in serenity is one
of the wisest investments that one can make.*

*I took this seriously. Just as I spend money to purchase all
the things that I need and want, and feel good about being
able to do so, I am in the process of viewing any loss as a
beneficial purchase. The amount lost is what I pay to
acquire serenity.*

82

Every Detail Exact

$\int$ ome people feel a strong need for each detail to be exactly right. This often causes them needless stress.

In some fields even small details are highly important. For a surgeon a tiny detail may mean the difference between life or death. For an airplane pilot a minute detail can make the difference between a safe landing or a fatal crash. But in most instances small details will not make a significant difference. Being excessively concerned about trivial details can be a source of much distress.

Be serene when you think about details. Planning a wedding, a banquet, a convention, an important meeting, or a festive meal for guests, you might want everything to go exactly right. You want each detail to be just so. This can enhance the occasion. But do not allow this attention to detail to ruin your health, to precipitate anger and quarrels, or to create needless stress. Handling details that do not go the way you wish with serenity can be more impressive to those you wish to impress than having each detail exactly right.

If you are excessively concerned about details, analyze why you have such a strong need. It may be because you feel your self-image is on the line. Remember that your value is a given and you do not need to have each detail perfect to have worth and value. It could be because you fear the disapproval of others if something goes wrong. It could be because you want the honor and glory and praise of people saying, "All the details were just right." Even if you find pleasure in this, it is more beneficial for your total well-being to be serene whether or not you are praised. It could be that this is how you grew up and it just seems to you that this is the only proper way for things to be. Even if you do consider this an absolute necessity, there is an even greater necessity to be serene. In short, whatever your motive for wanting details to be exact, it is wise to have an even stronger motive to be serene.

"I have several relatives who used to dread special occasions which required planning and preparation on their part," the elderly grandmother related. "I loved these occasions."

"What do you consider the core difference why you felt positive about them and those who felt differently?" she was asked.

"I haven't really given this a lot of thought," she said. "But now that you ask me it seems to me that those who experienced excessive levels of nervousness and stress wanted everything to go exactly right. I, too, want things to go

right. But I have had enough life experience to know that often details will be out of my control. Power failures can happen at inopportune moments. Someone who should have shown up does not arrive on time. Misunderstandings happen. I take this in stride. I don't feel a need to prove to anyone that I'm perfect. I know I'm not, and it's all right if others see this. The benefit of this attitude is that I enjoy preparing for special occasions."

83

Infuriating Comments

*I*t is easy to become irritated, upset, even infuriated over irrational, mistaken, judgmental, or biased comments made by others. Some people replay these statements in their minds over and over again. They were distressed the first time they heard them, and each time they mentally replay the dialogue, it increases and prolongs the stress they experience.

To master serenity we need to develop calmer attitudes toward statements and opinions we feel should never have been said. We cannot control the thoughts expressed by others. It is difficult enough to control our own words. It is impossible to make certain that no one will write or say things that we feel are religiously, politically, or personally off track. It may be appropriate to be a bit upset for a relatively short period of time. But if it persists for much longer than appropriate, you will be preventing yourself from being serene. Your mind will be occupied with distressing thoughts and you will not be making the wisest use of your brain and your time.

Learn to let go and shift your focus to beneficial thoughts. If you feel that by expressing your opinion those who made the infuriating remarks will reconsider and agree with you, it makes sense to do so. Disagree with the views, opinions, and perceptions of others with a centered and focused attitude and state. When you disagree angrily or vehemently, the person you disagree with is unlikely to say, "You have expressed yourself so angrily, now I will agree with you." What is more likely, the person will defend his position and become angry with you in return.

At times you might feel that even though the other person is unlikely to change his views, you need to express your counterview to let him and others know where you stand. By expressing yourself serenely, you are being dignified. This certainly will not diminish your chances of being heard.

Some people enjoy making comments to provoke others. They derive a sense of power when others protest their remarks. The best way to handle this is to maintain your serenity and calmly remark, "I differ with that." This understatement is often sufficient.

There are several writers of opinion articles that would get me extremely riled up. "How could they say that?" I would think to myself. I would repeat their nonsense and outrageous comments to others. And each time I repeated them, I myself was spreading their stupidity.

"How come this doesn't bother you as much as it bothers me?" I asked a friend of mine.

"I realize that people like this enjoy the illusory power their articles give them. If you don't take them too seriously, you rob them of their ability to bother you. In a day or two hardly anyone will remember what they wrote. Brushing off their drivel and pomposity is the most intelligent thing to do."

84
The Art of Viewing Objectively

There is an art to viewing objects, people, and situations objectively. This means that you see things as they "are" without any judgment. Practicing this from time to time will give you other serene experiences.

Our brain automatically makes judgments. "This is good." "This is bad." "I like this." "I dislike this." "This is awful." "This is wonderful." "This is pleasurable." "This is painful." "This is tremendously valuable." "This is a disaster."

Through doing this our brain helps us accomplish and make wise choices. It helps us avoid dangers and problems.

Problems arise when we needlessly view people, events, and situations in ways that cause stress and anxiety. Even if one is not able to view something positively, learning to view things objectively prevents distressful feelings.

If something takes longer than you would have wished, view it objectively: This is taking as long as it takes. If the weather is different from that which you would prefer, view it objectively without complaints: The weather is what it is. If a person does not speak to you the way you would wish: This person is speaking the way he does. Definitely if we can influence someone to speak more pleasantly, it is proper to do so. But by viewing the situation objectively, we will be much calmer about it.

When you practice viewing things objectively, you will gain a stronger awareness that stress is caused by negative evaluations. The more difficult you find it to view things objectively, the greater your need to practice.

When telling people to practice objective observation, those who are strongly negative often present arguments to defend their right to be negative.

"But if I'm objective, I'll make many mistakes," they say.

"If you are consistently negative, you'll make even more mistakes," they are told. "When you need to take corrective action or avoid problematic situations, your brain will let you know. Observing objectively does not mean regressing to infancy without the ability to exercise good judgment. It means that you don't counterproductively get upset by non-dangerous occurrences and situations."

I watched someone descend from an intercity bus. As he walked down the steps, he turned to the bus driver and thanked him, "You got me here not a moment too soon, and not a moment too late. The timing was exactly right." This man was a regular on that bus, and one could tell that this was his habitual response. By viewing the actual outcome as the way things should be, he was able to maintain a consistently calm and upbeat state.

85

If Not Now, When?

The great Sage Hillel used to say, "If not now, when?" Hillel is telling us not to push off until tomorrow what we can do today. If you don't study now, when will you study? If you procrastinate, later on you will also push things off in the same way that you are pushing things off now, and never get around to it. So study, now. Take action, now. Help someone out, now.

This wisdom applies to serenity. There will always be reasons why it is difficult to be serene. There are always things to take care of. There are always problems to solve. There are always factors to focus on that will make it difficult to be serene. Challenging situations are always happening. So if you feel that, "Now I can't be serene," when will you be serene? The same way that now it is difficult to be serene, when "later" becomes "now" it will still be difficult, albeit for a different reason. So the only way to master serenity is to think of "Now."

"Now is the time to be serene." And the more difficult it is at a given time to be serene, the greater your mastery of serenity by being serene right then and there. So instead of justifying a lack of serenity, make the internal mental effort to be serene anyway. By doing so, whatever difficulties you are facing at a given moment will become a bit lighter.

There is yet another aspect to what Hillel is telling us. My teacher, Rabbi Chaim Mordechai Katz, the late Rosh Hayeshivah (Dean) of Telshe (Cleveland), frequently commented on this, "Sometimes you really have a valid reason for not being able to study right now. If so, when will you study? That is, right now make up a specific time when you study. If right now you can't do an act of kindness for someone, make up a specific time when you will do that act of kindness. The same can apply to serenity. If right now it seems to be totally beyond your abilities to be in a serene state, when will you be serene? Mentally visualize yourself being serene a bit later. This could be when the noise that is bothering you stops. This could be when you take care of a pressing matter that is weighing heavily on your mind. This could be when an especially challenging person walks away. By clearly defining when you will be serene, you will be able to access some part of that serenity right now.

I am the type of person who experiences the present fully. When I am joyous, I feel as if I have always been joyous and always will be joyous. An issue for me is that when I am in a distressed emotional state, I feel as if this will last forever. It was suggested to me that even when I am experiencing a large degree of stress and tension, I should visualize myself being serene later on when things settle down. This has proven very helpful for me. Even though now I am not yet serene, I have a vision of being serene a little later. This takes a large part of the edge off the present.

86

Before Sleep

*B*efore you fall asleep at night and when you wake up in the morning, your brain is in a state called alpha state. The brain waves are slower than when you are in the normal waking state called beta state. In alpha state, your brain is more open to positive suggestions than when it is in beta state. Utilize this to make suggestions that you will increase your ability access and maintain serenity.

As you fall asleep at night, repeat to yourself a few times, "I will sleep serenely. I will have serene dreams. I will experience greater serenity tomorrow and in the future." This is a wonderful time to visualize yourself being serene.

Parents of young children can make suggestions to their children while they are about to fall asleep that they will have serene dreams and that they will wake up serenely and will experience serenity the next day. This should be said in a calm, slow, soothing tone of voice. Older children who are open to this will likewise benefit it. But it is counterproductive if they become annoyed. However, those who realize the power of these suggestions before sleep will appreciate them greatly.

I tend to be a worrier. When it was totally quiet just prior to my going to sleep at night, my worries would hit me. They made me anxious and I had trouble falling asleep. I was advised to use this time as an opportunity to build up my level of serenity. I was told that all I needed to do was speak to myself soothingly and tell myself that I am going to become a serene person. This was one of the most effective tools that I have ever learned. Not only did it save me from loss of sleep and much anxiety, after keeping this up for a number of months it transformed me into becoming a generally serene person.

87

What's Your Approach to Life?

*Y*ou have two basic paths to choose from in life. One path leads to anxiety and stress. The other path leads to serenity.

The path of stress means that you view situations and circumstances with frustration, anxiety, worry, nervousness, fear, hysteria, or panic. There are numerous levels of stress. But the general approach is one of distress. This prevents clear thinking. Some situations fall into the category of being able to improve, change, or solve, but because of the stress one's mind is stuck and does not see what is obvious or what could be discovered with creative thinking.

The path of serenity means that you view each situation with a calm attitude. Your initial reaction might be one of distress, but you think thoughts or take actions that calm your mind and muscles. Whatever situation arises will be there regardless of whether you are stressed or serene. Accessing a serene state enables you to think clearly and creatively. You might think of ways to improve the present reality. Even when you cannot, your inner calm enables you to cope with the challenges at your best.

Even before you have found the optimal way of using your mind when you are faced with challenging situations, just knowing that you have the potential to view it serenely will make it lighter and easier to deal with. This is similar to the perspective of, "This, too, shall pass." Knowing that your distress is temporary enables you to feel better about it. You find it easier to access your inner strength, courage, and elevated thinking.

Develop the habit of asking yourself about situations, "What way of looking at this would help me handle this more serenely?" There are always many ways to look at a situation. There are ways that build your character, ways that are elevated, ways that are courageous, ways that are humorous. Develop your creativity and you will think of ways that work for you.

Be aware of your present approach to life. Be totally committed to choose the path of serenity over the path of stress. Keep moving forward. If you reflect on your path and feel that you are not yet on the path to serenity, do not fret. At that very moment you can make a new choice. You can choose to walk the path of serenity. And you can choose this right now.

88

Verses for Serenity

*H*ere is a selection of verses from *Psalms* that will help increase serenity. The translation is from *The Stone Edition Tanach*.

- "You, Hashem, are a shield for me, for my soul, and the One Who raises my head." (3:4)
- "I fear not the myriads of people deployed against me all around. Rise up, Hashem; save me, my G-d." (3:7,8)
- "When I call, answer me, O G-d of my vindication. You have relieved me in my distress; be gracious to me and hear my prayer." (4:2)
- "Let the light of Your face shine upon us, Hashem." (4:7)
- "In peace, in harmony, I lie down and sleep; for You, Hashem, will make me dwell solitary and secure." (4:9)
- "All who take refuge in You will rejoice, they will sing joyously forever, You will shelter them; and those who love Your Name will exult in You." (5:12)
- "I will thank Hashem will all my heart, I will proclaim all Your wondrous deeds. I will rejoice and exult in You, I will sing praise to Your Name, Most High." (9:2,3)

- "And those who know Your Name will trust in You, for You have not forsaken those who seek You, Hashem." (9:11)
- "But as for me, I trust in Your kindness; my heart will exult in Your salvation." (13:6)
- "Protect me, O G-d, for I have sought refuge in You." (16:1)
- "I have set Hashem before me always; because He is at my right hand I shall not falter." (16:8)
- "Hashem is my Rock, my Fortress, and my Rescuer; my G-d, my Rock in Whom I take shelter, my Shield, and the Horn of my Salvation, my Stronghold." (18:3)
- "May Hashem answer you on the day of distress." (20:2)
- "Hashem is my Shepherd, I shall not lack. In lush meadows He lays me down, beside tranquil waters He leads me. He restores my soul. He leads me on paths of righteousness for His Name's sake. Though I walk in the valley overshadowed by death, I will fear no evil, for You are with me. Your rod and Your staff, they comfort me." (23:1-4)
- "My G-d, in You I have trusted, let me not be shamed." (25:2)
- "Hope to Hashem; strengthen yourself and He will give you courage, and hope to Hashem." (27:14)
- "Hashem is my Strength and my Shield, in Him my heart trusted and I was helped; and my heart exulted, with my song I praise Him." (28:7)
- "For my Rock and my Fortress are You, for Your Name's sake guide me and lead me." (31:4)

- "You are a shelter for me, from distress You preserve me; with glad song of rescue You envelop me." (32:7)
- "As for one who trusts in Hashem, kindness surrounds him." (32:10)
- "Our soul longed for Hashem; He is our Help and our Shield. For in Him will our hearts be glad; for in His Holy Name we trusted. May Your kindness, Hashem, be upon us, just as we awaited You." (33:20-22)
- "Who is the man who desires life, who loves days of seeing good? Guard your tongue from evil, and your lips from speaking deceit. Turn from evil and do good, seek peace and pursue it." (34:13-15)
- "Hashem is close to the brokenhearted; and those crushed in spirit, He saves." (34:19)
- "For with You is the source of life; by Your light may we see light." (36:10)
- "Praiseworthy is the man who has made Hashem his trust." (40:5)
- "May they rejoice and be glad in You, all who seek You." (40:17)
- "Cast upon Hashem your burden and He will sustain you." (55:23)
- "In G-d I have trusted, I shall not fear." (56:5)
- "Trust in Him at every moment, O people! Pour out your hearts before Him; G-d is a refuge for us." (62:9)
- "For You are my Hope; O Lord Hashem, my Security since my youth." (71:5)

- "I will say of Hashem, '[He is] my Refuge and my Fortress, my G-d, I will trust in Him.'" (91:2)
- "He will charge His angels for you, to protect you in all your ways." (91:11)
- "Come! Let us sing to Hashem, let us call out to the Rock of our salvation. Let us greet Him with thanksgiving, with praiseful songs let us call out to Him." (95:1,2)
- "Sing to Hashem a new song; sing to Hashem, everyone on earth." (96:1)
- "Serve Hashem with gladness, come before Him with joyous song." (100:2)
- "Sing to Him, make music to Him, speak of all His wonders. Glory in His Holy Name, may the heart of those who seek Hashem be glad." (105:2,3)
- "Give thanks to Hashem, for He is good, for His kindness endures forever." (107:1)
- "This is the day Hashem has made; let us rejoice and be glad on it." (118:24)
- "Please, Hashem, save now! Please, Hashem, bring success now!" (118:25)
- "You are my G-d, and I will thank You; my G-d, I will exalt You." (118:28)
- "I raise my eyes upon the mountains; whence will come my help? My help is from Hashem, Maker of heaven and earth." (121:1,2)

- "May there be peace within your wall, serenity within your palaces. For the sake of my brethren and my comrades, I shall speak of peace in your midst." (122:7,8)
- "Every day I will bless You, and I will laud Your Name forever and ever." (145:2)
- "Hashem is close to all who call upon Him, to all who call upon Him sincerely." (145:18)
- "Let all souls praise G-d." (150:6) This is the last verse in *Psalms* and on this verse the Midrash states that we should praise the Almighty for each and every breath. Those who do this frequently will live a serene life.

89

Collect Serene Moments

$\mathcal{R}$ecord any or all of your serene and joyous moments. Write down instances and places when you were especially serene. Afterwards as you read your list you will once again access those states. Keeping this list will make you more aware of new serene moments as they arise. When you remember contexts when you have already been serene, this will help you access those serene states in more and more contexts.

_____

_____

_____

_____

_____

_____

_____

_____

_____

_____